THE TRAIL

—— TO ——

SUCCESS

A City Manager on Leadership, Management,
and Civic Empowerment

HOWARD W. BROWN JR.

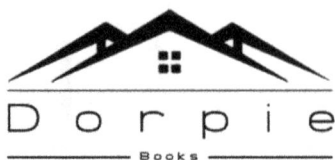

2024 DORPIE BOOKS, WASHINGTON, D.C.

www.dorpiebooks.com

Library of Congress Cataloging-in-Publication Data

Brown Jr., Howard W.

The Trail to Success: A City Manager on Leadership, Management, and Civic Empowerment/Howard W. Brown Jr. — First edition.

Pages cm

ISBN: 978-0-9996794-2-5

1. Brown, Jr., Howard, 1971 – 2. Brown, Jr., Howard, 1971 – 3. Business Management – 4. Business Memoir – 5. Government Leadership

To my loving mother, Juanita Funderburk-Vasile, and my cherished grandmother, Emma Kittrell, whose selfless devotion and countless sacrifices were the lifeblood of our family. Every page of this book is a testament to the profound impact of your love and proof that your labor was not in vain.

CONTENTS

PROLOGUE

TO THE SURPRISE OF MANY, my journey to becoming one of the youngest and few Black city managers has deep historical roots, tracing back to the Muscogee people and the rise of the Seminole tribe. Their fierce resistance to territorial encroachment in Florida, coupled with their alliance with the Black Seminoles, has inspired me since my childhood in Pensacola. The Seminoles and their African American allies faced down slaveholders and military forces through three grueling wars, marking the longest Native American conflicts in US history. Their unyielding defense of their lands resonates with me.

At my alma mater, Florida State University, I channeled the Seminole spirit into my public administration studies, aiming to make a societal impact. My career took off in Escambia County, a region marked by Andrew Jackson's conquest and the remnants of Seminole settlements.

The biggest milestone in my career came in Oklahoma, when I was hired to lead a city named after Muscogee survivors of the Trail of Tears. That brutal chapter in American history bore witness to the suffering and deaths of thousands of Native Americans and African Creeks who would join with Black Muskogeans to make significant contributions to the civil rights movement.

Understanding the history and culture of the places I've served is crucial to my approach, even learning Spanish to better connect with the communities. My appointment as Muskogee's youngest and first Black city manager is a testament to the progressive mindset of the predominantly white elected officials. This same spirit of inclusivity and advancement paved the way for my groundbreaking roles as the first Black city manager in Bell, California, and as the pioneering city manager in Indiantown, Florida.

While studying at the Harvard Kennedy School, I had the opportunity to reflect on the evolution of city management. I'm struck by its transformation since the early 1900s. The profession has come a long way since the earliest city managers were hired during the era of women's suffrage and Jim Crow. Despite progress, African American representation in this field remains low, highlighting the ongoing need for change.

My path through management was marked by financial constraints and learning on the job, rather than through formal training. Discovering the International City/County Management Association later provided much-needed guidance. I share my story to illuminate the path for civil service managers and to help citizens understand the lives of public servants.

Personal and professional challenges have shaped my career. The end of my marriage and financial struggles early on, criticism in the media, and being blamed for policies beyond my control have tested me. Yet, like the Muscogee, I've remained resolute and hopeful. It's my desire that my story will inspire the same resilience in others.

INTRODUCTION
- PENSACOLA, FLORIDA

Growing up in Pensacola, Florida, the precariousness of my circumstances was never more apparent than during the oppressively humid summers. At ten and seven, my brother Rodney and I would often find ourselves lounging around in worn underwear, seeking respite from the heat in front of a droning electric fan. We'd while away the hours absorbed in television while eating sandwiches made with government cheese. To pass the time and entertain ourselves, we would engage in an ill-advised game with our mother's old pistol. I'd playfully snatch it from my underwear and point it at Rodney, jokingly threatening to shoot.

"I'll blow your brains out!"

"Not unless I blow yours out first!"

Our youthful naiveté blinded us to the genuine peril of our circumstances.

The image is indelible in my memory—strutting through the house, pistol in hand, aiming it squarely at Rodney's head while making careless threats. In hindsight, it's unfathomable that an accidental twitch of a finger didn't irrevocably alter our lives. Our emergence from those reckless episodes unscathed is nothing short of miraculous.

We relied heavily on government assistance to get by. With a mother disinclined to cook, the only proper meals we could count on were the weekend repasts at our grandparents' home. There, our doting grandmother would ply us with hearty dishes of meatloaf and fried catfish. Beyond those brief respites, we subsisted on the provisions allotted by food stamps and the meals provided at school. I find myself wishing that those who advocate for the dismantling of such programs could understand the vital lifeline they extended to us and so many other children for whom school lunch was the closest thing to a reliable source of nourishment. That safety net instilled in us a deep respect for the government institutions that kept us afloat.

My grandparents, especially my grandmother, were our primary caregivers. Granddaddy, an older man, was generally kind but was also prone to fearsome displays of temper. I still vividly recall the time he flew into a rage upon discovering that Rodney and I had devoured the baked chicken and rice his wife had prepared for supper before he had a chance to eat. In his inebriated fury, he cobbled together a meager sausage sandwich only to hurl it in my face as retribution for our perceived insolence.

But it was our grandmother who imbued our turbulent home with a much-needed dose of tenderness and stability. She cared for our grandfather with saintly devotion as his health declined precipitously due to unchecked diabetes, an affliction that would eventually claim his lower extremities. All the while she cooked, cleaned, and tended to his daily needs, she never failed to assure us grandchildren that we were welcome to anything in her house.

When my grandfather passed away during my seventh-grade year, my mother decided that Rodney and I should live with my grandmother full-time. She continued to nourish us, body and soul, with wholesome meals made possible by the modest earnings from her cleaning jobs. By this point, Rodney and I were pitching in to help with her biggest weekend gig—a formative experience that taught me the value of hard work and gave me a window into the adult world far beyond my years.

Every Saturday at the crack of dawn, like seriously around 6 a.m., we'd head to the expansive Zulu Grand Hall catering facility to ensure it was spotless in time for the day's events. I quickly learned that punctuality was non-negotiable—even a moment's tardiness meant a mad scramble to finish our work under the judgmental glares of arriving guests.

With military precision, I would painstakingly scour my assigned half of the hall while Rodney mirrored my efforts on the opposite end. No crevice was spared our attention—at an age when most of our peers were still mastering the art of playtime, we were entrusted with the formidable responsibility of ensuring every surface gleamed and not a speck of debris marred the floors we had polished to an impeccable sheen. I would maintain this grueling routine without fail until I finally left home for college.

My grandmother imparted to me the cardinal rules of gainful employment: punctuality is sacrosanct, integrity must be beyond reproach, all instructions are to be followed to the letter, and no question is too trivial to ask for clarification. Her unwavering standards made it abundantly clear that anything less than consummate professionalism was anathema. To this day, my grandmother's uncompromising standards reverberate through every aspect of my professional life.

In addition to our work at the Zulu Hall, Rodney and I would accompany her on housecleaning assignments in the homes of the well-heeled where we'd wash their cars and mow their lawns. There I quickly grasped the immense trust these families were placing in us. Even a whisper of impropriety, like a misplaced tchotchke, could result in swift and irrevocable termination.

We never got paid directly for helping Grandma, but she would reward our hard work with a few treats during our weekly trip to Barnes Supermarket. Rodney would stock up on Chips Ahoy cookies, milk, bologna, and bread. My picks were Oreos, fruit punch, and a ham-like mystery meat. Although I'm not sure when or how we figured it out, we knew not to bother with flimsy junk food like Now and Later candies. Watching my grandmother stretch those lean times into moments of joy taught me so much about resilience and grace under pressure.

As high school approached, I started itching for my own spending money. I picked up jobs at places like McDonald's, but the real opportunity came the summer I was selected for a program that placed at-risk students in professional work environments. Through the program, I landed a gig at the downtown Pensacola employment office.

I already knew how to be a good employee thanks to Grandma, but there was just one problem—I needed professional clothes. With no other options, I made do with an old, ill-fitting white suit jacket handed down from my older brother. It was a double-breasted style that had long since gone out of fashion, and to make matters worse, underneath the jacket I wore a golf shirt and tie. I must've looked ridiculous.

Under the watchful eye of my supervisor, Mr. Felton Bryant, I began to learn the ropes of the employment world. As a high school student on the cusp of adulthood, my knowledge of such matters was understandably limited, but Mr. Bryant took it upon himself to guide me through the intricacies of the job with a patient hand.

One day, as I sat observing Mr. Bryant counsel a particularly nervous job seeker, I got an unexpected lesson in the real-world consequences of personal choices. Mr. Bryant explained to the man that a prospective employer had been impressed by his performance on a forklift operator's test, but ultimately declined to hire him because he had been drinking before the interview.

The man sheepishly admitted he'd had a beer to calm his nerves, so desperate was he to land the job. Mr. Bryant turned to me and asked if I had any questions for the applicant. Without thinking, I blurted out, "Man, why did you have a beer? My grandmother said you can have a drink after work."

The man hung his head in shame and said simply, "I don't know. I was just nervous."

My heart broke for him. In that moment, I understood more deeply than ever how even small choices can have major ripple effects in our lives. It was a lesson in personal responsibility I would never forget.

Around this same time, my brother Rodney graduated high school. We were so close, it almost felt like we were graduating together. Rodney may not have been a star student, but he had an incredible work ethic and a lot of common sense. He had such a big influence on me that when he enlisted in the Navy, I had a feeling I would end up following in his footsteps in a few years.

When I turned sixteen, procuring a driver's license became a coveted rite of passage, but this modest ambition was a challenge due to the $10 license fee. After countless hours practicing in Grandma's car, she agreed to front the money for my first road test. I failed—not once, not twice, but three times in a row. It was beyond humiliating. My mom washed her hands of the whole thing, insisting it was on me to find a way to make it happen.

But my grandmother, a woman of indomitable grit and grace, took me aside and reaffirmed her steadfast belief in my capacity to triumph. She assured me that no matter how lean the times, she would gladly dedicate a portion of her next paycheck to giving me another chance. Her willingness to quite literally invest in my success, even at the cost of her own comfort, left an indelible mark on my psyche.

That license opened up my world in ways I could never have imagined, including the night I met the future mother of my children at a party on the other side of town. Elle was fair skinned with long thick hair and a tiny hourglass body. She was the prettiest girl I'd ever seen. She was a high school freshman and only allowed to attend the mostly upperclassmen gathering because it was hosted by her next-door neighbors. The connection between us was instantaneous and undeniable. From that moment on, we were inseparable outside of school.

Elle's family was better off than mine. Her mom was a homemaker and an excellent cook, so I gladly accepted every dinner invitation that came my way. Her dad, the family breadwinner despite his advancing age, took on a fatherly role in my life. I was fairly close with my own father, but his job had recently relocated him to Jacksonville.

When I wasn't with Elle and her family, I was usually with my best friend Jason. To this day, I don't think I've ever had a truer friend. Jason was such a good friend, he'd often swing by the Zulu hall to help me finish up my work there.

Our friendship dated back to sixth grade at Brentwood Middle School, but we grew especially close in ninth grade. A big part of that was the fact that we had a level of independence and freedom of movement that was rare among our peers. We both had older brothers who served as parental figures, which meant no curfews and minimal oversight. But we never really got into trouble. We spent most of our time bouncing between friends' houses and biking all over the city, getting into some typical teenage mischief but nothing too serious.

Jason's mom had such a nurturing spirit, and I loved being around her. She welcomed me like a second son from day one. Our family status was cemented when our families realized they'd grown up in and around the same low-income housing complex called Morris Court.

While my brother Rodney was a major influence, it was ultimately my friendship with Jason that altered the course of my life. More specifically, it was Jason's older brothers who had gone to college that planted the idea in my own head. I didn't have any other college role models in my family or social circle. Jason's brother Gerald had played baseball on an athletic scholarship at a school in Alabama, and his oldest brother Philip was an Army officer and a member of Alpha Phi Alpha fraternity. They were the ones who introduced me to ideas like picking a major, choosing a college, and finding ways to get school paid for.

Jason had his heart set on Florida State University, about a two-hour drive from Pensacola. I had never been to Tallahassee, but I decided to apply there too. We even hatched a plan to join the National Guard reserves together using the buddy system.

Thanks to years of athletics, I took to the physical demands of basic training like a fish to water. In no time, I was setting records on the fitness tests and attracting the attention of my commanding officers.

My boy Jason struggled to keep up and got relegated to remedial fitness training. But he never lost his sense of humor about it, even when I teased him about being in "fat boy boot camp."

My first few years of college were a blur of football games, dorm pranks, and frat parties. Long before I had any idea what it really meant to be an "Omega man," Jason had his sights firmly set on pledging Omega Psi Phi Fraternity, Incorporated. His enthusiasm was contagious, and I soon found myself swept up in the excitement.

When the day of the big interest meeting finally arrived, I squeezed into an old double-breasted suit that Grandma had bought for me years earlier. It was snug in all the wrong places, but I stood tall as I introduced myself to the brothers, regaling them with stories of my Pensacola roots and rattling off my accomplishments. I was brimming with confidence, even as I silently prayed the seams of my suit would hold together. Jason had to miss the meeting due to some family issues, and he ended up not pledging during college.

But I did pledge, and my fraternity brothers quickly became some of my closest confidants and allies. Chief among them was Ben Crump, who would become the renowned civil rights attorney. Even back then, Ben had a commanding presence and a sense of purpose that seemed to hint at his future path. As the dean of our pledge class, he set a high bar and inspired us all to be our best selves.

Junior year brought an unexpected twist when Jason decided to drop out of school and stay home after Christmas break. It caught me completely off guard, and I nearly followed suit.

Jason and I had been renting a cheap trailer in a mobile home park, but without his half of the rent, I was in a serious bind—I couldn't afford to stay, but I also didn't have the cash to break the lease. In a panic, I called up my high school buddy Mark, who was a year ahead of us at FSU. I asked him to drive me back to Tallahassee so I could clear out my stuff. I explained that on top of being short on rent, I had missed the deadline to apply for next semester's financial aid.

Mark, ever the wise and mature voice of reason, was quick to set me straight, saying mine was a bad idea. He reminded me that we shared a name and a bond, always calling each other "Junior" as a nod to the fact that we were both named for our fathers.

"Junior, so what are you gonna do?" he asked pointedly.

"I'm going back home, Junior," I said with a sigh.

"To do what?" he pressed. "Sit in Granny's house?"

His words hit me like a bucket of ice water, but I still didn't see a way out of my predicament. That's when Mark threw me a lifeline. Turns out, one of his roommates had just graduated, leaving an empty bedroom. Without hesitation, Mark offered to front me the $4,000 I needed to get out of my lease and pay my tuition for the coming semester. I could pay him back once my financial aid came through.

I returned to FSU in January with a renewed sense of purpose. Not only was I more comfortable in Mark's nicer digs, but living with him and his roommate gave me a firsthand look at what it took to be a serious student. These guys were pulling down nearly straight As, and I quickly saw why. They had organized notes, flashcards, practice tests—the works. By following their lead, I watched my own grades turn to As as well.

I ended up completing all my undergraduate coursework by the fall of senior year. Mark, in his infinite wisdom, told me I could use my remaining financial aid to get a jump on grad school if I held off on formally graduating. So I marched into the department chair's office and got permission to enroll in three graduate courses—public administration, government personnel management, and an overview of public sector professions.

Around this time, I got some more exciting news. Elle and I had continued to see each other when I came home. After Christmas break, we learned that she was pregnant. In a moment of youthful impulsiveness and ardent devotion, Elle and I eloped. We drove to the courthouse in Tallahassee, our hearts full of hope and trepidation, and pledged our lives to one another.

I was overjoyed to have a beautiful wife and a son on the way, but the reality of providing for a family was just starting to sink in. Most of my friends were either heading to graduate school or had landed impressive jobs. Ben was off to law school, and my line brother Ali had snagged a job with an elite consulting firm. I knew I needed to keep pace, so I set my sights on a master's degree.

I applied to the graduate program in public administration at the University of West Florida, and to my great relief, I was accepted. Even better, they offered Elle and me a spot in their family housing complex, which was a godsend for nontraditional students like myself.

And so, Elle, our young son Clint, and I settled into life at the UWF family housing complex. We were surrounded by other students who, like us, were juggling the demands of academics and parenthood. It was a tight-knit community built on shared experiences and mutual support—a place where we could chase our dreams while still tending to the responsibilities of family life.

Even then, I knew this was just the beginning. I had no illusions about the road ahead—I knew it would be marked by both triumphs and challenges, breakthroughs and setbacks. But I felt ready to face whatever lay around the bend. I was armed with the knowledge and skills I had worked so hard to acquire, buoyed by the love and support of my family, and fueled by a determination that had been forged in the crucible of my early life.

Looking back on that time, I can't help but marvel at how seamlessly the pieces of my life seemed to fall into place. From my academic achievements to my whirlwind marriage to Elle, from my acceptance into grad school to the opportunity to live in family housing—each step along the way felt touched by the hand of fate. It was as if some unseen force was guiding me, propelling me forward toward a future I could only begin to imagine.

1

ESCAMBIA COUNTY, FLORIDA, THE BEGINNING

IN THE SUMMER OF 1995, I found myself on the cusp of a significant milestone: graduation from the University of West Florida's MBA program. The faculty and staff there had been incredibly supportive, enabling me to work full-time in the Department of Student Affairs, where I provided academic counseling, and on weekends, I administered standardized tests like the SAT and LSAT. This arrangement also afforded my family the convenience of living in graduate housing on campus.

I needed to earn six internship credit hours to complete my degree. About twenty of us who'd formed a tight-knit academic community and were now poised to graduate competed for just three internships. Dr. Larry Walker, the internship coordinator, played a pivotal role in guiding me through this process.

As part of the preparation for my interviews, Dr. Walker briefed me on the expected dress code, a crucial aspect of making a good first impression. Of course, I knew from my previous jobs at the employment office and as a National Guard reservist how to dress, but Dr. Walker, one of those lovable, bleeding-heart liberals, was concerned about something else.

He delicately said to me, "Howard, do you mind if I offer you a bit of advice that might be a little upsetting?"

I said sure, and he went on to ask nervously, "Can you cut your hair and take those earrings out?"

At the time, I wore a giant cubic zirconia in each ear lobe and walked around with my hair in a five-inch-high top fade like I was auditioning to be the third member of Kid 'n Play.

Dr. Walker's comments came during a particularly fraught era in which the hot topics of the day were the efforts to outlaw affirmative action in California college admissions and "The Bell Curve," a controversial book that insinuated the intellectual inferiority of certain racial groups. These circumstances heightened my sensitivity regarding my Black identity, and I didn't want to allow my fashion choices to become another arena for judgment or stereotype.

I took youthful offense at Dr. Walker's request and insisted my outside appearance has nothing to do with my intellect. I tactfully let him know I thought he was on some nonsense; however, circumstances being what they were, I then acquiesced.

On the day of my interviews, I first visited the City of Pensacola City Manager's office. Because I didn't want to risk the bus being late, I arrived exceedingly early and was able to observe my peers, Jerry and Tammy, as each exited their interview. Both had an easy rapport with the manager, leading me to feel uncertain about my chances, especially considering Tammy's striking appearance and academic excellence.

Next, I faced the challenge of getting to my interview with the Escambia County Department of Planning and Zoning amid a torrential downpour. By the time I arrived, I was soaked to the bone. My clothes were clinging to me, and the squelching of water in my shoes was audible with every step. As I waited, the dampness began to take its toll. My clothes started to smell sour as my deodorant disintegrated under my arms. I was a mess!

Despite these setbacks, I found glimmers of hope. A Black woman senior planner was present alongside the department director. My academic focus on growth management, which is closely related to urban planning, seemed to resonate with the department's objectives, and I felt a connection with the senior planner that made me think I might just have a chance.

Weeks later, I returned to Dr. Walker to discuss the interviews and my concerns about not being selected. I candidly shared my fears that racial bias might have influenced the selection decisions. This suggestion visibly unsettled Dr. Walker.

He said, "Howard, that's not fair and not true. You haven't heard from them because they contacted the university. I've spoken with both Pensacola City and Escambia County, and both want you as their intern."

I said, "Stop playing, Dr. Walker!"

I was stunned because this felt like such a lucky break. I had never before been on the receiving end of such advocacy and support. I nearly cried with gratefulness, pride, and relief.

Dr. Walker recommended that I accept the internship with Escambia County Planning and Zoning, citing their track record of offering permanent positions to their interns. I accepted the offer, grateful for the wage of $7 an hour, and embarked on what would be the first step in my professional journey. I'd already had my first big epiphany: the challenge of overcoming preconceived notions.

This ground-floor opportunity at the Escambia County Planning and Zoning Department was a stepping stone to serving the public interest. Balancing the need to support my family with the desire to work in my field of study, I recognized the dual benefit of this role. It was here that I honed the skills of inquiry, analysis, and reporting—skills that would serve the community and shape my professional journey.

Understanding the importance of first impressions has been a cornerstone of my professional development. With a history of short-term jobs and military service, I was well aware of their significance. However, this internship represented more than just another job; it was the gateway to my career. The stakes were higher, the expectations more stringent, and my new boss would likely be less forgiving. This demanded a heightened level of dedication and performance from the outset.

Today, I advise young professionals to do their due diligence before starting a job, but in the mid-1990s, thorough company research prior to interviews or job commencement was a challenge. The internet was not yet the ubiquitous resource it is today. Despite growing up a mere ten blocks from the Escambia County offices, I had never set foot inside. This underscored the importance of putting my best foot forward.

As a graduate intern, my first month was a deep dive into the organization's culture. Building relationships in the workplace is a multifaceted endeavor, essential for career growth. While some may opt for social lunches to foster these connections, my financial limitations meant that lunch hours were spent working at my desk rather than dining out. Fortunately, I was assigned an office where interactions with colleagues were frequent and revealing. Casual conversations often veered into personal territory, with inquiries about my educational background and other details. These exchanges were not just pleasantries; they were opportunities to learn about the interpersonal dynamics within the department.

It quickly became apparent that opinions about my boss were polarized. While some colleagues expressed their dislike and skepticism, others were positive about her. These differing perspectives painted a complex picture of the leadership and the tasks at hand. Heeding my grandmother's advice—that with two ears and one mouth, I should listen more than speak—I adopted a posture of observation and attentiveness.

This posture allowed me to be privy to the undercurrents of office politics. Disagreements between coworkers were not just noise; they were insights into the challenges and alliances within the organization. This information was invaluable, teaching me the delicate art of navigating workplace relationships while remaining neutral.

My strategy was clear: avoid office cliques, focus on my assignments, and seek constructive feedback. By demonstrating reliability and a strong work ethic, I aimed to transcend my entry-level status and secure a permanent position. I understood that success in this environment was not just about completing tasks but also about understanding the nuanced opinions on how things should be done. This lowly internship turned into a masterclass in professional acumen.

I had the great fortune to be assigned to a senior manager named Michelle Andrewein, who had worked in New York. She was professional, sharp, and well-educated, and I was fortunate to be guided by her expertise. Our one-on-one time was not merely supervisory; it was an intellectual partnership. Together, we engaged in deep thought and strategic planning, akin to the rigorous analysis one undertakes when crafting a thesis. She oversaw long-range city planning, which required a methodical approach, setting us apart from the more immediate, hands-on tasks of departments like building inspections or law enforcement.

My initial project was instrumental in the creation of the Community Redevelopment Agency (CRA), which intended to utilize alternative financing methods to fund the revitalization of existing housing stock, the creation of new affordable housing options, and the promotion of mixed-use developments, in addition to fostering new commercial ventures.

The first big step in this endeavor was to survey housing conditions in the designated area that was plagued by neglect. Michelle and I ventured out into the community with tax maps in hand, developing a ranking system for the houses we assessed—ranging from one for the best conditions to five for the worst.

The raw data we collected from the field needed to be transformed into meaningful statistics. One area in which recent college graduates often have an advantage is in understanding new technologies. I did this here. Leveraging my proficiency with Quattro Pro, a precursor to Excel, I analyzed and presented the data, which culminated in a comprehensive report. This report was later reviewed and approved by the county's governing body, marking the successful completion of the project.

Throughout this process, the importance of asking the right questions and seeking clarity, a lesson ingrained in me from working with my grandmother as a teenager, was reinforced. Getting feedback is crucial to avoiding the pitfalls of rework. In those early days, when computers were not as prevalent, this meticulous approach was even more critical.

The report I helped produce was crucial to fulfilling the agency's mandate. The fruits of our labor are evident today in the enhanced infrastructure and commercial growth within the area now known as the Warrington Revitalization Area. Residents can now observe new sidewalks, the arrival of popular establishments like Chick-fil-A, Lowe's, and Target, and other visible improvements. These developments are a direct consequence of the groundwork laid by the CRA at its inception in 1995 and showcase the lasting benefits of strategic urban redevelopment.

In line with Dr. Walker's foresight, my internship evolved into an opportunity for a permanent role. A vacancy emerged for a zoning inspector, a title subsequently upgraded to Code Enforcement Officer II.

I was set to start after my internship ended in August of 1995; however, my National Guard unit was activated after Hurricane Erin struck Florida. I was deployed for several months but made it home in October. I was relieved because it allowed me to be at the birth of my daughter, Cierra, the following month.

Interestingly, the US Bureau of Labor Statistics reports that government employees tend to be more educated than their private sector counterparts, often possessing qualifications that exceed the requirements of their roles. This was certainly true in my case, as the position did not necessitate a college degree, yet I held a master's. Despite this apparent overqualification, the role offered a tangible benefit: it included a company car. Given that our family was managing with just one vehicle, the addition of a second car promised considerable convenience.

My tenure as a Code Enforcement Officer was immensely fulfilling. My responsibilities included verifying that citizens' actions aligned with their applications, ensuring property maintenance, and enforcing zoning laws. My job's impact was evident—the community was cleaner, safer, more orderly, and aesthetically more appealing. From instructing someone to mow their lawn or dispose of inoperative vehicles to shutting down businesses operating in prohibited areas, I found myself naturally adept at encouraging property owners to adhere to local codes and ordinances.

The entire code enforcement department was led by Danny, who had a reputation for exceptional leadership and expertise. In addition to being a good leader, he was a beacon of knowledge, holding certifications in every inspection trade within the state. At first, I didn't understand the significance of such extensive qualifications, but a glimpse into his office, a veritable shrine to his achievements, revealed the depth of his commitment and proficiency. His colleagues affectionately dubbed him "Mayo with nine lives," a moniker that spoke to his resilience and indispensability.

My immediate supervisor was Cecil Williams. He required all of his reports to meet daily at Smokey's for lunch, where we bonded over half-priced pork sandwiches, fries, and sweet tea that only cost $2.50, which I could now afford. This was part of Cecil's strategy to foster team unity.

Cecil was easy to work with; however, in contrast to Danny, his knowledge of the procedural processes of the department was limited. His background as an environmental enforcement officer, with roots in law enforcement, meant he lacked Danny's comprehensive understanding of the statutes that governed code enforcement. He was not adept at showing me the ropes of administrative tasks like writing citations.

As a consequence of Cecil's ineptitude, I faced a steep learning curve with the establishment of the code enforcement department. Before its establishment, code enforcement was handled haphazardly by either the billing department or the police department, with the latter sometimes arresting individuals for severe violations. Consequently, I found myself having to learn the nuances of my role independently, navigating the complexities of code enforcement without the full guidance I had anticipated. The problem was exacerbated because our office lacked written policies and procedures related to code enforcement.

Rather than complain, I took the initiative and spearheaded the creation of a citation program, strictly adhering to state law and county ordinances—a first of its kind. Before this, interpretations of statutes and codes varied widely, leading to stagnation. My policy and procedure for issuing citations became the standard that is still followed today. My understanding is the manuals I created twenty-five years ago are still being used.

Moreover, I was the pioneer in obtaining inspection warrants, a task that others found daunting. I vividly recall preparing my first inspection order, presenting it to the duty judge, and being sworn in. My documentation was thorough, citing reasonable cause based on observed violations and interactions with property owners. This diligence paid off when, despite a homeowner's refusal, we were able to execute the warrant with the sheriff's assistance, even in the face of resistance.

That day, as I stood with the sheriff while he handcuffed a defiant homeowner, over two dozen of my colleagues witnessed the enforcement of the law, a moment that underscored my leadership. It was clear that leadership is not just about holding a position; it's about setting an example, pioneering new paths, and earning the respect and endorsement of your peers. This experience was a defining moment for me, solidifying my understanding of what it truly means to be a leader.

As my comfort and confidence grew, I consciously embraced a growth mindset and took a proactive stance in my professional role. This led me to achieve certification across three levels of formal training offered by the Florida Organization of Code Enforcement. The knowledge and skills I acquired allowed me to settle into my daily routine with ease, and I began seeking opportunities to enhance my contributions. I actively assisted my colleagues and eagerly volunteered for key projects, demonstrating my commitment to the team's success.

One area in which I did not excel was in setting boundaries. This is something that, in hindsight, I realize is crucial in preventing burnout and preserving a healthy balance between my work and personal life. As it was, my service-oriented mindset intensified, I forced myself to give more and more to our citizen customers, my superiors, and my peers alike.

Eventually, this backfired.

As I settled into my role, it was clear that my proactive approach and initiative did not sit well with everyone.

On one occasion, during one of our quarterly staff meetings that had to be held in an auditorium, I overheard an argument between two people who were senior to me. Initially, I was unable to hear the details but could clearly see some intense finger-pointing and shouting going on.

Curiosity piqued, I strained to listen and managed to catch a pivotal moment in the argument. When one said to the other, "You're just pissed because Howard Brown is a whiz kid."

I was shocked. I couldn't believe these two very grown people were having an argument about my low-level self. The incident would portend the rough waters to come. For the time being, however, I just felt a little puffed up as I made the transition from code enforcement to the demolition team.

In this capacity, my colleagues in code enforcement would refer cases to me, indicating properties ready for demolition due to noncompliance by the owners. Collaborating closely with the attorney, we would present these cases to the Unsafe Structures Board to secure demolition orders. My role was comprehensive: coordinating with road crews for the physical demolition, liaising with utility companies to disconnect services, ensuring proper disposal of debris with the landfill, and meticulously inventorying the contents of each house to safeguard against future claims. This attention to detail was crucial, as it protected us from potential disputes, such as claims of valuable items like a $5,000 baby grand piano being destroyed without record.

I found a great deal of satisfaction in my demolition job, particularly because it offered the benefit of unlimited overtime, and I was fortunate to have colleagues who were remarkably easygoing. However, the work environment was not without its challenges; the supervisors could be unpredictable, and job security was tenuous, as dismissals were not uncommon.

During my initial years on the job, I navigated these challenges without incident. But in 1999, my circumstances took a turn for the worse when I fell out of favor with one of my superiors. As a form of retribution, I was transferred to a project located in the most remote part of the county. This reassignment added a burdensome forty-five-minute commute each way to my daily routine and, in retrospect, signaled the onset of a downward trajectory with Escambia County, and my personal life as well.

2

ESCAMBIA COUNTY, FLORIDA, THE FAREWELL

TOWARDS THE END of my time working for Escambia County in Florida, my personal life began to unravel. It started with the dissolution of my marriage to Elle. We had gotten married far too young, and our differences proved insurmountable. With two toddlers at home, my wife struggled emotionally while I juggled three demanding jobs—for the county, part-time at Sears, and in the National Guard Reserve.

I had no idea how to be a good husband. My parents weren't married, and my grandfather was in a state of deterioration during my formative years. I remember once, in a misguided attempt at a thoughtful Mother's Day present, I gave her cleaning supplies and a vacuum. I really told myself this was to help HER. But of course, I was just being stupid.

Amidst all this chaos, I picked up smoking cigarettes to try to relieve the stress, a habit I hadn't touched since college. Looking back, I'm actually surprised I didn't start smoking earlier, considering how common it was for students to light up during dorm room hangouts over beers back in my undergrad days. I can still vividly recall those first tastes of cigarettes in college at McCullum Hall. Crowds of students would gather on weekends, chain-smoking and drinking beer. That's where I first picked up the occasional bummed light, though I didn't buy my own. I might go a week or more sometimes without one before the next chance presented itself. The nicotine addiction crept up on me gradually as stresses mounted over the years. What started as sporadic social smoking morphed into a daily pack habit to cope with the chaos of young family life and nonstop work.

By the final grueling months of grad school, compounding pressures drove me to start heavily smoking. Juggling academic demands, fatherhood to little Clint and Cierra, and multiple jobs to keep us afloat financially, cigarettes became an unhealthy crutch. My pack-a-day habit continued for nearly a decade.

When I took a job with the county after earning my master's degree, they paid me a paltry $16,000 per year. That measly salary wasn't nearly enough to support my new family, so I scrambled to take a second job at Sears selling computers and car audio systems. Every other weekend was eaten up by National Guard reserve duties on top of that.

Municipal government jobs are notorious for low wages. Studies find public employees with college degrees make 4–11 percent less than similarly educated private sector workers. For positions needing some college but no degree, local government pays nearly $12,000 less on average than the private sector. So for about seven years, I worked seven days a week juggling the county job, Sears, and the National Guard to barely keep our heads above water.

My Sears gig did have its upsides though. I enjoyed the commission-based sales and got to build on my budding interest in computers and technology. The interpersonal side of retail was a natural fit for me too.

I kept at it for so long mainly for the decent supplemental income it provided on top of my paltry government salary.

But overall, the grind was incredibly draining and demoralizing. I was killing myself working up to sixty hours some weeks for the county on top of my other jobs. I'd be out the door before sunrise for the forty-five-minute commute, put in my ten hours, then race to Sears to clock in from 5:30–10 p.m. Fitting in Guard duty one weekend a month was yet another responsibility competing for my time. I took no vacations and never called out sick. If I did take leave from the county, I'd spend the day working at Sears instead just to make a little extra money. My life revolved around endless cycles of commuting, inhaling meals, and hopping from one shift to another with no reprieve.

It was beyond frustrating that all my hard work earning a master's degree had still landed me in a paycheck-to-paycheck struggle requiring an utterly exhausting schedule. But I had growing expenses and kids to feed, so I did what I had to do to keep the lights on and food on the table. But one undeniable fact was that I was passionate about my job in local government. I believed in it. The motivations of public sector employees often differ starkly from private sector workers. While companies can dangle profit-sharing and stock options, civil servants tend to be driven more by an intrinsic desire to serve the greater good.

As if financial strain and overwork weren't enough, my work superiors proved to be more than human, and favoritism and bias became problems. One manager would praise me to my face but then tank my job prospects by giving scathing secret references. Another supervisor punished me harshly for exposing his friend's unethical behavior. This crony would loot homes for valuables like TVs and copper pipes before demolition crews tore them down, which I reported upon discovering.

In retaliation, my manager banished me to the most rural, conservative sector of the county.

As the lone Black code officer there, I endured relentless disrespect and hostility from residents aghast at a Black man wielding authority in their neighborhoods. Slanderous complaints about me poured into our office, which my supervisor leveraged to make my life hell. But I knew from prior experience that speaking up would be futile.

Shortly after I started with the county years earlier, I once confronted a white coworker for using the n-word slur. He had the audacity to deny it and claim he said "African American" instead. Another colleague privately confirmed hearing the slur to me but wouldn't back me up publicly for fear of retaliation himself. So I filed an official complaint, only to have it dismissed as no big deal, with zero consequences for the offender. It drove home that in this conservative enclave, casual racism went largely unchecked.

Sadly, the stress fractures in my marriage with Elle stemmed from fundamental incompatibility from the start. Marrying too hastily in our youth before understanding ourselves or our goals, we could never quite get on the same page. She routinely undercut my professional aspirations, culminating in one pivotal disagreement over the Sears management training in Birmingham.

Steven Richards, my manager at Sears, was really impressed with me and shared that he wanted to recommend me for management. The only problem was it would require me to relocate temporarily to Birmingham, Alabama, for a training program. I was excited about the possibility of making more money managing weekends and evenings at Sears with the possibility of continuing in this role in another city if I relocated for a better opportunity in city government. But Elle refused to consider relocating, insisting if I attended the training, she'd pack up the kids and move back in with her widowed mother. She belittled my "dead-end" professional ambitions, urging me to just go work with her brother at the railroad instead.

Her response typified her pattern of failing to support my goals if they didn't align with her own wishes. She hadn't attended college and was blind to the opportunity in government. The marital strain compounded the pressure from my intense work-life juggling act, with the county government jobs serving as our primary income alongside my Sears side hustle. Elle's lack of understanding only magnified my stress levels.

Ultimately, that period proved to be the darkest chapter of my life. I had to face the fact that I wasn't going to be able to overcome the problems in my marriage or escape the combination of grueling hours, cronyism, and my biased work environment with limited promotion potential. I accepted the hard truth: for the sake of my career ambitions and emotional well-being, I would need to make the agonizing choice to leave behind my family and hometown to seek out brighter horizons elsewhere.

Around this time the internet was exploding, and a company called Monster.com launched with a media blitz that illustrated this new way of finding a job anywhere by doing a job search online. I jumped at the chance, sprucing up my resume and applying to postings. I managed to land a role as Chief Code Enforcement Officer for the city of Lauderdale Lakes in South Florida, my ticket out and first supervisory position.

Though I couldn't see it yet, finally prioritizing my own needs would unlock the next level. What felt impossible in the moment later emerged as the crucial turning point that altered my trajectory for the better.

In retrospect, I credit my survival in those early days to steadfast commitment to hard work, reliability, perpetual growth, and cultivating allies. Those values fostered resilience as I weathered each challenge. I emerged more dedicated than ever to upholding integrity and ethical leadership in local government. The handful of bosses I witnessed who prioritized an organizational culture of accountability earned my deepest respect and emulation, even as I paid a personal price. Professionally, I gained hard-won experience in government operations and political machinations.

3

LAUDERDALE LAKES, FLORIDA

DIVORCE IS NEVER EASY. The emotional toll can be devastating, and for me, it felt like my world was crumbling around me. I thought my move to South Florida would give me a fresh start professionally and emotionally, but this wasn't the case. As I grappled with the reality of not living with my kids full-time, I became consumed by worry over how this would impact their development. The trauma ran so deep that even overhearing a woman complain about her partner would trigger an explosive reaction from me.

I vividly recall having breakfast with colleagues one morning when a woman mentioned her boyfriend wasn't being a good partner. I immediately went on the defensive, interrogating her about whether he was out at nightclubs or cheating on her. When she clarified that he was just working too much, I erupted into a tirade of insults, swearing never to speak to her again. Looking back, it's clear I had a lot of unresolved anger and pain from my own failed marriage that I was projecting onto her innocent remark.

It was the late 1990s, and online dating was just starting to take off, particularly in the Black community with the rise of BlackPlanet.com. I was sharing an apartment with my fraternity brother Richard, a former NFL draft pick who had transitioned into law enforcement. While I wasn't using the site consistently, I did go on a number of dates through the platform, with varying degrees of success.

On one particularly memorable encounter, I had connected with a woman on BlackPlanet who, based on her profile, seemed to be a very attractive woman. In our chats, I'd learned that she was also successful working as a dentist or pharmacist. We agreed to meet up at a local CVS, and I even had Richard on standby to call me with an excuse in case I needed to make a quick exit.

When I arrived, I parked and waited to see her car. She pulled up in an enormous Ford Excursion, and I immediately noticed she didn't quite resemble her photos. More critically, when she got out of her SUV, she towered over the car and must've been at least six feet tall. I'm while I stand at a more modest 5'8" and I wasn't trying to be Deuce Bigalow. Not wanting to waste either of our time, I made the split-second decision to speed away, leaving her standing there in astonished disbelief.

There were other disastrous "dates"—the woman who turned into the Incredible Hulk when her omelet arrived slightly overcooked, the one who left her young kids at home alone while she joined me for drinks, and the one who turned out to be the girlfriend of one of my fraternity brothers!

These wild and often unpleasant post-divorce dating experiences quickly soured me on the singles scene, and I decided to focus on my career. I had just landed my first management position as the Chief of Code Enforcement for the city of Lauderdale Lakes. The timing was fortuitous, as the city was undergoing a transition from a council-led system to a council-manager form of government. This shift involved establishing a dedicated code enforcement division, which I would be leading as its inaugural chief.

It was a significant step up in my career but also a daunting challenge. I was now responsible for overseeing a full staff of code enforcement officers, housing inspectors, and other personnel, despite having no prior supervisory experience or training. There were no established standard operating procedures to follow, no institutional knowledge to draw upon. I had to build everything from the ground up while learning on the job.

One of my first moves was to bring on board Gerald Henry, a seasoned code enforcement professional from the larger Broward County organization. Gerald was an educated family man with a stellar track record in the field. While some might have been intimidated to hire someone so knowledgeable, I saw it as an opportunity. Gerald brought cutting-edge ideas and best practices that elevated our work and made us a highly effective team.

Together, Gerald and I tackled the biggest issue facing our division: the proliferation of poorly maintained properties across the city. Overgrown lawns, dilapidated houses, and other eyesores were dragging down neighborhood appearances and property values. We quickly realized that the worst offenders were predominantly rental properties with absentee landlords.

To address this, Gerald devised a brilliant solution: a comprehensive rental housing inspection program. Under this initiative, every single rental unit in the city would undergo an annual inspection for code compliance and proper maintenance. A small $68.50 per-unit fee would be assessed to cover the program costs.

The potential benefits were enormous. Not only would it generate over $2 million in much-needed revenue for the city each year, it would also drastically improve the quality of life for renters and the aesthetic appeal of our neighborhoods. By having our existing code enforcement officers conduct these inspections as part of their regular duties, with a dedicated rental inspector to oversee the program, we could achieve maximum impact with minimal additional resources.

The program was a resounding success in its first year. Thousands of violations were identified and delinquent properties were brought up to code, and the revenue rolled in. However, our success also put us in the crosshairs of landlords and apartment associations who chafed at the increased scrutiny and regulation.

They hired lobbyists to undermine our efforts, arguing that we were overstepping our authority. They claimed that under state law, municipalities could not inspect rental properties with more than four units, as that was the exclusive domain of the state's Department of Business and Professional Regulation.

While our legal counsel assured us we were well within our rights, the political pressure took its toll. After just a year, the city council caved to the special interests and terminated the program, citing concerns over potential lawsuits to recoup the fees. It was a frustrating setback, watching a program with such profound positive impact fall victim to the power of money in politics.

Despite its short-lived existence, the rental inspection initiative showcased the incredible value that employees like Gerald can bring to an organization when given the opportunity to innovate. It reinforced a key leadership philosophy for me: always strive to hire people who are smarter than you and possess skills you lack. When you empower talented individuals and grant them the autonomy to put their ideas into action, they can achieve remarkable things.

Gerald went on to have a highly distinguished career, eventually returning to Broward County as its director of code enforcement. I will be forever grateful for his contributions during his time on my team, and for the lessons he taught me about the power of smart, strategic hires.

Of course, not every personnel decision I made was as successful as bringing Gerald on board. One of the toughest challenges I faced early on was having to fire an employee for the first time. Maria had come to the US fairly recently from Puerto Rico, and while she never revealed this to me, in retrospect, I suspect she didn't have reliable transportation. She was habitually late to work. At first, I tried to be accommodating, telling her to call me when she was running behind so I could have someone cover the phones until she arrived. My intention was to be a nice, understanding boss.

However, her tardiness soon became a daily occurrence, to the point where I was essentially doing her job in addition to my own. I realized I needed to be firmer, so I sat her down and told her directly that she needed to be on time going forward. What I failed to consider was the potential for miscommunication due to language barriers.

The very next day, she waltzed in late again. When I confronted her, she became irate, reminding me that I had told her to call if she was going to be late. In her mind, I had given her blanket permission to arrive whenever she pleased as long as she notified me. I was flabbergasted.

It was a hard lesson in the importance of clear, unambiguous communication, particularly when managing a diverse team. I should have been crystal clear, stating something to the effect of "It is mandatory that you arrive by 8:00 a.m. sharp every day unless there is a verified emergency. Is that understood?" By trying to avoid sounding harsh, I had inadvertently created confusion.

I gave her an official warning, explaining in no uncertain terms that any further tardiness would result in termination. Lo and behold, she was late again the next day. I had no choice but to follow through on my word. Even though I liked her as a person, I had to put my feelings aside and do what was necessary as a manager. We both shed tears in my office that day.

Having to fire someone, especially for the first time, is gut-wrenching. But it taught me a valuable lesson about leadership. You have to establish expectations plainly, document them in writing, and be willing to have difficult conversations when those expectations aren't met. At the end of the day, you have to let the employee's actions dictate the consequences. You can counsel, coach, and encourage improvement, but if there's still no progress, sometimes termination is the only option. It's never easy, but it comes with the territory of being a supervisor.

Not everyone on my team was thrilled with my newfound authority. I had one particularly hostile subordinate who went so far as to curse me out during a staff meeting. As a hot-headed twenty-something, it took every ounce of my self-control not to react with physical force. I sent him home for the day to cool off and issued an official reprimand. After he had a chance to reflect and realize how close he had come to being fired or even arrested, his attitude improved markedly. Again, I learned that sometimes a little compassion and restraint in the face of disrespect can go a long way.

As the chief of code enforcement, I quickly formed a close friendship with my coworker, Celeste, who was the community development specialist. Celeste was a few years older than I was and wiser still beyond her years. She had exceptional EQ and was nearly clairvoyant when it came to reading a room. Her judgment was always sound, and I learned to trust her advice.

When our former boss, Jesus, received a job offer to become the director of planning in a nearby town, he wanted to bring Celeste and me along as city planners. Initially, I was thrilled at the prospect of working with Jesus, who was an excellent boss, in a larger city. However, Celeste came to my office with a warning.

"Howard, listen," she said. "I'm not going with Jesus, and you shouldn't either. I grew up near there, and everyone knew not to be there at night." Her words carried a deeper meaning, implying that the town was not a safe place for Black people after dark, despite the fact that they might work there during the day.

Celeste continued, "Jesus is not going to be there long, and when he leaves, we'll be out of jobs."

Heeding her advice, I chose to stay in Lauderdale Lakes with Celeste. As she had predicted, Jesus left his new position in less than a year, validating Celeste's foresight and the wisdom of our decision to remain where we were.

One of my proudest accomplishments during my tenure at Lauderdale Lakes was uncovering a staggering $23 million in outstanding code enforcement liens owed to the city. I worked with my assistant to comb through mountains of case files and citation records to arrive at this figure, compiling the data into an extensive spreadsheet. When I presented my findings to the city council, it ended up making front-page news.

I was a bit too candid in my remarks to the press, openly criticizing the lax enforcement that had allowed these debts to accumulate prior to my arrival. My boss just chuckled at my naivete, gently advising me to direct all future media inquiries to his office. He recognized that I still had a lot to learn about politics and public relations, but he was willing to extend me some grace as I grew into the role.

One of the most terrifying days in American history occurred while I was working in Lauderdale Lakes on September 11, 2001, when planes flew into the World Trade Center towers, killing nearly 3,000 people. I called my ex-wife and asked her not to let the kids watch television because I didn't want them to see those innocent people jumping out of the burning buildings.

Although we were seemingly far away, our city was placed on high alert because, at the time, Lauderdale Lakes had a large Jewish community with a significant number of synagogues, and we were vigilant against potential local attacks.

I had not previously been a fan of then-President George W. Bush, but his visit to rescue workers, firefighters, and police officers working at Ground Zero really moved me. I remember him holding that bullhorn and yelling to the crowd, who had trouble hearing him.

"I can hear you! I can hear you! The rest of the world hears you," and then he said the words that make me shiver to this day, "And the people who knocked these buildings down will hear all of us soon."

Looking back, my time in Lauderdale Lakes was a crucible that forged me into the leader I am today. I was thrust into a management position with no prior experience, forced to sink or swim. I had to navigate challenging personnel issues, implement ambitious new programs, and establish my authority in the face of skepticism and outright defiance.

At the same time, I was struggling to regain my personal equilibrium in the aftermath of a devastating divorce. I was acting out in ways I'm not proud of, lashing out at innocent bystanders and engaging in ill-advised attempts at dating. It was a period of tremendous upheaval and growth, both professionally and emotionally.

Through it all, I learned invaluable lessons about leadership, communication, and perseverance. I discovered the importance of hiring smart, nurturing innovation, and standing firm in my convictions. I also gained a newfound appreciation for the power of empathy, both in managing a team and in relating to others on a human level. My experience in Lauderdale Lakes was a trial by fire, but it was also a turning point. It set me on the path to becoming the self-assured, principled leader I am today. And while I may have moved on to bigger and better things, I will always look back on that chapter with a mix of fondness, pride, and gratitude for the lessons learned and the relationships forged.

As I prepared to embark on the next phase of my career in Atlanta, I did so with a renewed sense of purpose and a hard-earned set of leadership skills. I knew that no matter what challenges lay ahead, I had the resilience, adaptability, and strength of character to overcome them. And for that, I will be forever grateful to the city of Lauderdale Lakes.

4

LILBURN, GEORGIA

AFTER A FEW YEARS living in South Florida, I started dating a woman who was a consultant based in Atlanta. After visiting, I felt that relocating there would be a good decision. The city was just a four-hour drive from Pensacola, which meant in addition to having my kids during the summer, I could see them more frequently throughout the year.

After researching openings, I applied for two positions that seemed closely aligned—the code compliance manager role with Gwinnett County government and the neighborhood improvement manager job with the city of Lilburn, which is one of Gwinnett County's smaller municipalities.

I went through the full interview process for both roles. For the county code compliance manager job, I instantly hit it off with the interviewer, Don Jasper, who was the department director. Don was extremely well respected in the local community. During our conversation, he mentioned that he was getting close to retirement age and whoever was hired for this role could potentially be in line for a promotion to replace him soon. That intrigued me, as upward mobility is always attractive. However, I also had the contrasting thought that if Don left, there could be major changes or disruptions under new leadership.

46

My interview for the city of Lilburn neighborhood improvement manager position went very differently. I met with Tom Comps, who was the city manager at the time. Tom came across as quite conservative but didn't strike me as being blatantly partisan or polarized. He seemed grounded in his personal beliefs while still being able to separate that from treating people of diverse backgrounds with respect.

After the interviews, I quickly received offers from both municipalities. I was actually leaning heavily toward the position in Gwinnett because on paper, Gwinnett seemed a better fit with more opportunities for advancement. The deciding factor in my decision was a brief yet revealing interaction with the Gwinnett County HR director. The director's curt and demeaning demeanor raised a red flag about the organizational culture. In any institution, the individuals placed in critical outward-facing roles serve as ambassadors, reflecting the values and attitudes of the leadership. If a city's HR director, responsible for managing the human capital and cultivating a positive workplace environment, displayed such hostility, it signaled deeper systemic issues within the administration. Recognizing these warning signs, I ultimately accepted the neighborhood improvement manager position with the city of Lilburn, where the leadership demonstrated a more respectful and inclusive approach, better aligned with my professional values and goals.

Atlanta was the perfect soil for me to put down roots and cultivate my best life, and I did just that. I quit smoking and purchased my first home in a predominantly Black suburb east of the city. For a young, driven man about town, Atlanta had it all—a robust social scene, booming businesses, and a multicultural renaissance shaping the New South. Those fast-paced times cultivated a refreshing live-and-let-live mentality.

The city was truly a mecca for Black professionals. However, I was living in the Decatur area of Atlanta at the time. It was an incredibly exciting period in my life—it felt like a nonstop reunion with my college friends from Florida State University in Tallahassee, as so many of them had also relocated to Atlanta. A fraternity brother, now a nationally recognized attorney, used to host "game night" get-togethers. The atmosphere was like a nonstop house party. As the host, I would cook up delicious soulful feasts in my crockpot—dishes like smothered chicken smothered in gravy over rice. Well, one night a recent Spelman College graduate showed up, bless her heart, thinking she could hang with our group, most of whom had over a decade of drinking experience under our belts. The kid, who was a young prosecutor for one of the local counties, passed out, and someone shouted for a doctor. To my surprise, there were three physicians in the room!

Those days, I relished inhabiting the Southern capital of cool, which Atlanta's first Black mayor, Maynard Jackson, once dubbed "too busy to hate"—a maxim that absolutely rang true. The city's energy was infectious, its stride outpacing any undercurrents of prejudice or small-mindedness.

When I arrived in Atlanta, Jackson's successor, Bill Campbell, was the mayor. I was familiar with him because he was a member of my fraternity, Omega Psi Phi. During his first term, Campbell made significant strides, including overhauling the city's finance department, passing a major bond issue to fund infrastructure improvements for the 1996 Summer Olympics hosted in Atlanta, rebuilding the public housing system, and modernizing the legal, public works, and water departments. Remarkably, violent crime rates also dropped notably under his leadership.

Campbell, who'd attended Vanderbilt University and Duke University Law School, was hailed as a new breed of "post-civil rights" Black politician. He capitalized on Atlanta's economic renaissance, built a diverse coalition of voters, and was viewed as a potential future US senator or governor of Georgia. Pundits likened Campbell to Barack Obama before Obama's rise, as a pioneering African American political figure with crossover appeal.

However, Campbell's tenure became marred by a five-year federal investigation into possible corruption during his mayoral administration. In 2004, he was indicted by a federal grand jury on charges of racketeering, bribery, wire fraud, and tax evasion.

While ultimately acquitted of the racketeering, bribery, and wire fraud charges, on March 10, 2006, a federal jury convicted Campbell on three counts of tax evasion. He was subsequently sentenced to thirty months in prison for those tax evasion convictions, tarnishing his once-promising political legacy. It was a reminder to me that public servants need to be impeccable in their dealings.

This new chapter was pivotal for my professional development thanks in large part to Tom, who was a former Navy officer and alum of UC Berkeley. By his example, I was able to start looking at myself critically. For example, I realized I needed to have stronger writing skills.

For the first time, I had a boss who was more than a mentor; he was a sponsor, which made a significant difference. Within just one year of me being in that role, the planning and zoning director position opened up. Tom and the outgoing director both agreed that I would be well suited for that job. The director who was leaving had previously worked in code enforcement himself. He thought people with that background tended to make great urban planners and zoning managers because we were trained to keenly analyze zoning laws, enforcement, and all the tiny details. So with his endorsement and Tom's support, I was promoted into the planning and zoning director role overseeing that entire department—which was a big step up in responsibilities.

Even though I expressed uncertainties about being ready for such a big leadership role, Tom kept assuring me I was absolutely capable. He became an incredible career sponsor who constantly pushed my professional development. Tom encouraged me to join two vital industry associations—the American Planning Association (APA) and the International City/County Management Association (ICMA). He then put all kinds of useful training opportunities right in front of me.

Tom encouraged me to join professional organizations like the American Planning Association and the International City/County Management Association (ICMA), which offered extensive training opportunities. ICMA also allowed me to see the power of networking and how you can learn about opportunities that can dramatically improve a city.

Tom had been right. The International City/County Management Association (ICMA) offered valuable training opportunities.

My time in Lilburn gave me the trifecta in training. Throughout my fifteen-plus-year career in local government, I've found that success comes from a combination of formal education, job training programs, and on-the-job experiences. Each played a vital role in my professional development.

My master's in public policy provided the theoretical foundations in urban planning, public finance, policymaking, and statistical analysis. Core classes and case studies taught me to critically analyze issues like affordable housing, transportation, and economic development strategies. Concentration courses covered municipal management best practices.

However, it was the real-world learning that happened once I became a code enforcement officer and later a community development manager that truly prepared me. Senior colleagues taught me the nuances of diplomatically enforcing policies. I gained insights into redevelopment initiatives and navigating bureaucracy. As a supervisor, I learned to effectively manage personnel issues and get stakeholder buy-in for projects.

On the management side, experienced supervisors passed down wisdom about effectively managing different personnel situations— whether motivating an underperforming employee, tactfully resolving interdepartmental conflicts, or selling initiatives to get buy-in from key stakeholders. These were the invaluable soft skills developed through years of leading teams.

Conventions hosted by organizations like the Georgia Planning Association and American Planning Association offered workshops and networking that could be invaluable. Classes on public speaking, people management, using permitting software, or policy/procedure overviews would all help expand my skillset for this leadership role. As the department's public-facing representative, it was important for me to develop expertise in areas like conflict resolution, community engagement, and customer service.

The IRS left a lasting impression, teaching me the importance of integrating multiple perspectives and personal attention in management roles. To earn extra money, I worked part-time on weekends as a seasonal manager at the IRS, where I learned valuable management skills.

The IRS used a 360-degree performance review system created by Gallup, which incorporated feedback from supervisors, subordinates, and coworkers. This comprehensive evaluation method was eye-opening after working in high-performing local government roles. The IRS also conducted "departure evaluations" when employees left, similar to exit interviews, allowing the company to gather candid feedback about the employee's experience and perceptions of the workplace culture.

A transformative lesson came from feedback I received from a team member named "Latasha," whose name had an unconventional spelling and pronunciation. Mispronunciations of her name led to feelings of disrespect, and my default response of using last names to avoid issues inadvertently caused staff to feel disconnected and undervalued.

My manager coached me on the importance of learning to pronounce each person's first name properly. I committed to doing whatever was needed, including writing out phonetic spellings, sitting down with people to learn pronunciations, and consciously practicing. Taking the time to correctly say someone's name showed that I cared about them as individuals.

This experience taught me a powerful lesson about inclusivity and fostering an environment where everyone feels respected and part of the team. From then on, I made it a priority to pronounce all employees' names accurately, a small effort that made a big difference in building positive relationships.

Hurricane Katrina marked a period of unrest in Atlanta and in my life. Rain poured down across Atlanta, and in the Southwest area that is nearly all Black, they received a half foot of rain. An estimated 100,000 evacuees migrated to Atlanta, and an estimated 70,000 remain. Those people had nothing, and it was interesting to see how we responded.

The storm brought out the best in her city, even though it was hard to integrate 100,000 people in two weeks. There were stations set up for food, clothes, water, and shelter. Local schools enrolled students of all ages. It was wonderful to see the surrounding areas work together to help these families manage during the crisis.

Around this time there was also upheaval in my personal life. While in Atlanta, my kids who were still in elementary school would stay with me during the summers. I will never be able to thank my girlfriend at the time for the way she helped me care for the kids. Childcare would've bankrupted me, but I only had so much in vacation time. Sandy would use some of her vacation to help care for me. I don't know what I would've done without her, but unfortunately, I wasn't ready to get married again, and we ultimately broke up.

The constant positive was my job in Lilburn where I collaborated closely with the city manager to develop a comprehensive plan for the town's redevelopment and oversaw two huge and impactful projects. One was the building of a temple. When the Hindu community in Lilburn proposed building a temple on a 29-acre plot, they faced numerous challenges. As a city official at the time, I witnessed firsthand the hurdles they had to overcome.

The temple's proposed location, across from a busy commercial strip, raised concerns about traffic congestion. Some residents openly expressed their opposition to the temple, citing the Hindu faith as their reason. Additionally, the temple's spires exceeded the zoning district's height limitations, requiring a variance.

Despite these obstacles, the Hindu community persevered. They invoked the Religious Land Use and Institutionalized Persons Act (RLUIPA) of 2000, a federal law protecting churches from government overregulation. They even offered to pay a payment in lieu of taxes to demonstrate their commitment to the community.

As the city council deliberated, I found myself explaining the situation to concerned residents, emphasizing that the temple was being built on commercial property, not in a residential neighborhood. Ultimately, we couldn't deny the project, as federal law was on their side.

At the 2007 inauguration of the mandir upon completion of construction, a Vishvashanti Mahayagna was performed for world peace and family unity in the presence of over ten thousand people. In recognition of our efforts, Tom and I were presented with beautiful framed kalamkari, hand-drawn silk fabrics created using an ancient Indian art form. This gesture serves as a reminder of the importance of fostering understanding and acceptance in our communities.

Today, I am proud to report that the temple has become a featured attraction on Lilburn's website, a testament to the city's embrace of diversity. The Hindu community's dedication and willingness to work with the city played a significant role in this positive outcome.

The other major project I oversaw was a greenway trail system that would connect the city's beautiful parks. Lilburn had several lovely parks scattered throughout the four-square-mile community. However, it wasn't until we commissioned a consultant to survey the parks that we discovered an interesting feature: these parks were all connected by green spaces. This revelation was made possible through the use of aerial photography and GIS (Geographic Information System) technology, tools that were just beginning to gain traction in the public sector at the time.

Inspired by this discovery, we decided to capitalize on the existing green spaces and create an elaborate trail system that would link all the parks together. Our vision was to enhance the connectivity and accessibility of these recreational areas for the benefit of the community.

To bring this vision to life, we issued an RFP and selected a contractor and designer with the best plan for the trail system. The process involved real estate acquisition and some property condemnation to ensure successful implementation. The work Tom Combiths and I started in 2002 laid the foundation for what has become an elaborate trail system connecting these parks.

To fund the initiative, we sought grant opportunities and were informed by the Atlanta Regional Commission about a $1.2 million Greenway Trail Grant. We promptly applied and were thrilled when our application was approved, allowing us to proceed without burdening Lilburn's citizens with the cost.

The greenway trail system enhanced park connectivity and community pride. Through technology, regional collaboration, and innovative planning, we improved our town's quality of life without burdening taxpayers, exemplifying creative problem-solving and strategic public investments.

A decade later, I was amazed to see our fully implemented plan, demonstrating the power of communities defining goals, committing to long-term plans, and executing consistently despite leadership changes.

Despite Tom's encouragement and the positive trajectory he put me on, I eventually hit a professional ceiling in the small municipality of Lilburn. During a strategic planning session, both an outside facilitator and Tom recommended promoting me to assistant city manager. However, the city council bluntly shot down the idea, with one member stating, "We don't need another damn city manager!" After this, Tom suggested we both update our resumes. Although he didn't leave, I recognized I had hit a career ceiling and decided to seek a planning director role in a larger city. Tom was a pivotal mentor who transformed my career trajectory, shaping my passion for urban planning and development. While I appreciate my formative years in Lilburn, I knew it was time to apply my skills at a bigger scope and scale.

Tom continued being a great friend and mentor to me even after I left Lilburn. Tom played a crucial role in supporting my journey to become a certified planner with the American Institute of Certified Planners (AICP). As I didn't hold a degree in the field, it was essential to demonstrate my relevant work experience. To demonstrate my experience, Tom wrote a lengthy, detailed letter outlining all I'd done with the Greenway project. AICP then granted me membership.

5

ALBANY, GEORGIA

WHEN I STEPPED into the role of Planning Director in Albany, Georgia, I was stepping into a moment. The city, with its sprawling oaks and murmuring streets, was buzzing with the kind of electric anticipation that comes when change is not just hoped for but is tangible. It was 2007 and Senator Barack Obama was painting the horizon with possibilities, his campaign a canvas of hope that resonated with every step I took in those municipal halls.

The journey from Atlanta to Albany was a convoluted trek, a series of backroads that wound through the heart of Georgia, each mile a reminder of the transition from the pulsing epicenter of Black culture to a more languid way of life. Leaving behind the vibrant tapestry of friends and the city's invigorating rhythm was a bittersweet farewell, a necessary departure after nearly a decade immersed in two of the nation's most dynamic urban landscapes. It was time to pause, to allow the frenetic energy to settle, and to embark on a new chapter.

Departing Atlanta also meant relinquishing my side hustle, a constant companion that had accompanied me since the tender age of ten or eleven. The managerial position for the City of Albany represented a significant shift, the first time in my life where I found myself singularly focused on one professional endeavor. The echoes of my past—the part-time jobs, the weekends spent cleaning alongside my grandmother, the juggling of Navy Reserve and student work-study commitments—all faded into the background as I stepped into the all-consuming role that demanded 60 to 80 hours of my undivided attention.

The initial months in Albany were marked by a sense of transience, as I found myself residing in a nondescript extended-stay building, its drab walls a stark contrast to the vibrant aspirations that filled my mind. When my children visited, they were relegated to the living room, a makeshift sanctuary in the midst of our temporary dwelling. While my financial situation remained modest, I had honed the art of managing my resources with greater finesse. The discipline of timely tax payments and maxing out retirement contributions had long been ingrained, but now I had mastered the intricacies of budgeting, strategically timing my visits to Nordstrom's half-yearly sales to acquire a few well-crafted suits and ties.

Al, my boss, embodied this new era. As my first Black boss, he wasn't just a mentor; he was a symbol of the barriers we were breaking together. His leadership style, tempered in the discipline of military service, carried the authority of someone who had navigated both battlefields and bureaucracies. Al hired me despite the reluctance of his other department directors, a decision that not only set the tone for my tenure but also marked him as a leader unafraid to act on his convictions.

During the interview process, I had the privilege of meeting Alfred Lott, the city manager who would become a pivotal mentor figure throughout my tenure. Al, an African American, was not only my first Black boss but also a powerful representation of the change that was sweeping through the city. His presence added a layer of significance to the experience, making it all the more impactful for me.

After the city manager's hiring panel ranked me as their top choice candidate, I also excelled in interviews with department directors and, crucially, residents. The residents overwhelmingly supported my hiring, ranking me as their number one choice as well. However, in a perplexing turn of events, the department directors placed me dead last among the candidates.

It was years later that Al confided in me the reasons behind the directors' hesitation. Two main factors had come into play. First, my relative youth at the time had caused unease among the older directors, who felt threatened by the prospect of younger, upstart leadership. But more significantly, Al revealed that the directors had taken issue with my habit of discussing broad industry topics, societal trends, and management insights from publications during staff interviews, rather than focusing solely on the narrow operations of the department I would be overseeing. By demonstrating a well-rounded perspective and thinking expansively, I had inadvertently ruffled the feathers of some of the more insular directors.

Fortunately for me, Al chose to override the directors' objections in his decision to hire me. In his eyes, keeping the public satisfied was of utmost importance, as they were the ones I would be serving directly as Planning Director. And with Al, as city manager, giving his approval, he saw no need to defer to the outdated preferences of a director circle intent on maintaining an insular status quo. Though he made his hiring decision through a participatory process, it was ultimately a unilateral choice, a testament to his authority as an executive.

Although Albany lacked the glitz and glamour of its more cosmopolitan counterparts, I found myself energized by the prospects of my career. Compared to the sprawling Atlanta Metropolitan Area, Albany was a quaint town, yet with its 75,000 residents it dwarfed the city of Lilburn where I had previously worked. The planning department was a behemoth, a complex operation that boasted a staff of approximately 67 individuals in those pre-technology days, an era before modern efficiencies streamlined the need for specialized roles like cartographers and surveyors. It was a formidable responsibility, overseeing this vast planning apparatus, but one that I embraced with a sense of purpose and determination.

When I arrived, it was a community that had fallen on hard times economically after manufacturing job losses in previous decades. High poverty and unemployment rates had taken their toll.

As the head of the planning, zoning, permitting, code enforcement, and economic development functions, my job was going to be critical for facilitating Albany's revitalization. One of the major challenges I faced when starting was that the city's zoning codes and development regulations were extremely outdated, stifling new investment. There was also a perception that Albany was difficult for businesses to navigate, with convoluted and opaque permitting processes.

Overseeing the planning department of Albany, I faced a unique set of challenges that came with living and working in the same city. My responsibilities encompassed a wide range of issues related to the built environment, including code enforcement, sign regulations, and general upkeep of the city's infrastructure. Upon taking on this role, I quickly realized that the problems I observed during my daily commute, such as litter-strewn streets, cluttered utility poles, and dilapidated buildings, fell under my department's purview. The realization that these issues were not being adequately addressed was both frustrating and overwhelming, as the desire to fix everything at once can lead to a form of self-inflicted pain and ultimately result in accomplishing nothing.

From Al, I learned the importance of adopting a strategic approach to urban management. He stressed the significance of setting specific, achievable goals and objectives on an annual basis, coupled with a well-defined plan of action to ensure their completion. This practice, although not widely adopted, is essential for making tangible progress in a complex urban environment. Rather than attempting to solve all problems simultaneously, it is more effective to identify one or two key issues that can be realistically addressed and focus on delivering results.

To prioritize my goals, I aligned them with the objectives set by the city council and the long-term plans for the city's development. By doing so, I not only experienced the personal satisfaction of seeing projects through to completion but also demonstrated to residents and my management team that these initiatives were direct responses to the feedback and criticism we had received from the public. This strategic approach allowed us to make a meaningful impact on the city, addressing the most pressing concerns while laying the foundation for future improvements.

One of my first big priorities was leading an overhaul to streamline and modernize our zoning and land use regulations. We spent months reviewing the codes line by line to identify antiquated or burdensome requirements. I formed advisory committees with developers, builders, business leaders, and residents to get input on desired changes. Ultimately, we reformed the codes to be more user-friendly while still maintaining standards appropriate for Albany's vision.

Hand in hand with updating the regulatory environment, I knew we needed to improve our customer service for any entrepreneurs or companies interested in investing in Albany. We launched a comprehensive review of our permitting procedures to identify pain points and redundancies. By cross-training staff and leveraging technology more, we were able to develop a truly one-stop-shop permitting center. Applicants could now have their plans reviewed and approved by all divisions simultaneously in the same location.

Economic development also became a key focus for my team. We formed collaborative relationships with state agencies, chambers of commerce, and local stakeholder groups to develop marketing materials that accurately portrayed investment opportunities in Albany. My staff and I hit the road frequently to pitch our city's business-friendly climate, incentives, and strengths like our riverside location and amenities.

Within my department's purview, I made it a priority to stay on top of the latest urban planning best practices. We sent inspectors and code enforcement officers to training regularly on areas like hazardous materials, sustainable development standards, and legal updates. My senior planners attended continuing education courses on skills like comprehensive planning, GIS mapping, and innovative zoning methods like form-based codes.

While Albany's economic challenges were still an uphill battle in those first couple years I was there, I'm proud that our planning and development services department was seen as a catalyst for progress rather than an obstacle. By prioritizing code reforms, customer service, business recruitment, and professional development, we helped shape an environment more conducive to public and private investment in Albany. It took a lot of hard work, but we played a key role in beginning to shift perceptions about our city's future.

From day one, Al demonstrated himself to be an exemplary leader by every measure. Beyond simply bringing me aboard, he consistently empowered me with diverse responsibilities and exposures that allowed me to rapidly build experience.

For example, when a controversy arose involving misconduct allegations against a high-ranking staffer, Al hand-picked me to conduct an impartial fact-finding investigation that needed to be completed over a single weekend. This was a sensitive issue, and I was just a couple months into my nascent tenure, yet Al gambled on granting me special operational control over the entire department during this probe.

My approach was to methodically interview all relevant parties, meticulously documenting everything through a brief yet comprehensively structured report. The document included an executive summary up front, followed by a section detailing the issue and context. I then outlined three separate recommended courses of action, laying out the respective pros and cons for each option before concluding with my specific advice.

When I arrived at Al's office to submit the report, he insisted I sit down so he could go over it with me in detail rather than just accepting it perfunctorily. As he was reading my description of one particularly gossipy employee who had been snidely referred to the city manager in an offensive manner.

Though widely feared as an uncompromising, strict boss who had swiftly fired three department heads upon arriving in Albany, Al actually displayed a keen self-aware wit. He chuckled, showcasing an ability to take constructive feedback in stride and not take himself too seriously.

Over and over, Al demonstrated the tremendous trust and respect he vested in my judgment. Other people noticed it as well. When a municipal executive feared he was going to be fired for misrepresenting his affiliation with law enforcement, he sought my assistance in advocating Al for leniency on his behalf. I advised him to appeal to Al directly. But after he did so, Al pulled me aside to get my personal take on what disciplinary action seemed appropriate.

I recommended suspending the person who had violated the rules for ten days and placing him on a performance improvement plan for six months—a pointed consequence befitting the infraction, but one that still allowed for rehabilitation rather than termination. Incredulously, Al later revealed to me that he had actually been prepared to fire the individual outright until I intervened with that mitigating disciplinary alternative. It spoke volumes about the exceptional deference Al showed my judgment calls. It made me proud that someone I respected so much felt the same about me.

When the employee reached out to thank me for essentially saving his career based on Al's admission that he had considered termination before my counsel, I had to clarify for the employee that Al alone deserved the credit for making that final benevolent decision to be more measured. But it was certainly humbling to realize just how much stock the city manager privately put into my recommendations behind the scenes.

The many anecdotes illustrated Al's forward-thinking embrace of collaborative leadership. He mentored me while cultivating my potential, rather than distrusting or undermining an up-and-comer from a younger generation. His approach represented the polar opposite of the ossified, territorial mindsets I would encounter from other longstanding staff, the most difficult of which was Tim Ellis.

Tim was like a relic from another time, an older white man whose roots were planted deep in the local soil, perhaps too deep. As the world around him shifted, Tim clung to the old ways with a mix of defiance and desperation. His resistance was not just to my leadership but to the changing face of our community, to the winds of change that were sweeping across the country itself.

Tim's strategies were almost Machiavellian; he was skilled in the arts of manipulation and deception, playing colleagues against one another and bending truths to maintain his dwindling sphere of influence. But as much as Tim was a challenge, he was also a project. I put him on a performance improvement plan, not out of spite but from a place of responsibility—to him, to the department, and to the broader vision we were all striving towards.

This was not an easy task. The plan was met with resistance, each meeting a battleground of wills. Yet, as the nation rallied around a narrative of hope and change, I found a reservoir of patience I hadn't known I possessed. Slowly, through persistence and the inevitable encroachment of new perspectives, Tim began to adapt. It was a grudging acceptance, marked not by grand gestures but by small concessions and, occasionally, reluctant acknowledgments of the new realities.

One of the most challenging personal situations I faced in Albany involved an employee named Tim, who oversaw all the building inspectors, code enforcement officials, and that whole division.

Tim grew up nearby and attended the local high school. Outwardly, he resisted the community's changing demographics and any influence perceived as external advocacy for reform—what I'll bluntly characterize as "fighting the power" of new leadership like myself.

From our very first interactions after I arrived, it was clear Tim did not respect my authority whatsoever. He would go out of his way to belittle me through passive-aggressive slights like unnecessarily calling me "boss" in a derogatory tone whenever he came to my office.

Despite my politely but directly requesting that he call me "Howard" to maintain basic professional decorum, Tim persisted with the "boss" comments which felt to me like obsequious insubordination.

When I conducted Tim's first performance evaluation after just a few months on the job, I intended to give him a good evaluation since I did not yet have a reliably long track record to gauge his work against. However, I did notice his job description required certification as a building code official through the International Code Council (ICC)—something he clearly lacked based on my review of his file.

Tim claimed the former director, Richard, had explicitly exempted him from that certification requirement given his decades of experience as a general contractor. But when I consulted that prior director to verify Tim's assertion, Richard flatly contradicted it—stating the certification was a mandatory minimum qualification for the role, with no exemptions granted whatsoever. It had just been difficult to get Tim to comply.

Upon relaying Richard's stance, Tim became visibly infuriated and rashly accused me of calling him a liar over the apparent miscommunication with the former director. Though I calmly reiterated verbatim what Richard had told me, stating I simply wanted to clear up the discrepancy, Tim just grew more agitated and could not control his emotional response. True to his established pattern, he reacted impulsively and began raising his voice, blowing up at being challenged on his lack of proper credentials.

Given Tim's insubordinate outburst, I ended up writing him up formally and placing him on a performance improvement plan—he now had six months to obtain the required ICC building official certification his role demanded.

Tim failed the certification exam initially. This forced me to make a very tough decision—though we lacked anyone internally who could immediately replace him in that crucial role overseeing building inspections and permitting, his outright refusal to fulfill the minimum qualifications appeared to warrant termination.

Before making that potentially severe call, I first looped in Al to thoroughly apprise him of the situation and get his perspective. I recommended giving Tim one final chance to pass the exam before pursuing firing, if only because of our staffing constraints at that moment. Al concurred with extending Tim a last opportunity, once again showcasing his willingness to thoughtfully consider and value my judgment rather than simply unilaterally overruling it.

Regrettably, Tim only compounded the situation by subsequently sending letters of complaint about his alleged "mistreatment" at my hands to every county commissioner and city council member. This unprofessional escalation of what should remain a straightforward internal personnel matter represented an inexcusable act of insubordinate conduct.

As a result, a meeting was convened specifically about Tim's case. It included Al, the mayor, the county commission chair, and county administrator. The mayor bluntly made the city's position clear—Tim could either take the necessary steps to obtain his required certification or take his skills and experience elsewhere outside of Albany's workforce. The municipality would absolutely not budge on upholding what was a reasonable, minimum requirement that Tim had repeatedly violated and raised an unseemly public stir over, instead of simply complying.

When Al divulged in that meeting that I had actually advocated giving Tim one last chance at redemption despite his grievance-peddling behavior, the chairman questioned my leniency until the mayor firmly reinforced that Al held ultimate authority to determine appropriate disciplinary actions as he saw fit. The unified stance sent an unambiguous message that I had the administration's full backing to hold Tim accountable to reasonable employment standards.

The protracted stress and public angst Tim's gross insubordination imposed peaked with an audacious phone call I received from his wife. In a display of shocking entitlement, she verbally attacked and hurled racist insults at me.

Despite Tim and his wife's animosity, the air was electric with the promise of change, a palpable sensation that even It was HOPE, a force that had propelled Barack Obama's campaign to victory, and as I sat in solitude before my television, witnessing history unfold as he was proclaimed the next president of the United States, I felt the boundaries of possibility expand before me.

Compelled by an irresistible urge, I soon found myself purchasing a plane ticket to Washington, DC, to bear witness to the first Black president of the United States, despite lacking tickets to any of the inaugural events. It was a pilgrimage of sorts, a journey I knew I had to undertake. Fortune smiled upon me when an old girlfriend, with whom I had maintained a close friendship, offered me a place to sleep on her sofa. As serendipity would have it, she was hosting her play mother, a prominent figure in Mississippi politics, who managed to secure an extra VIP ticket for me to some of the most sought-after events.

We found ourselves immersed in the grandeur of an inaugural ball at the Four Seasons, serenaded by the incomparable Aretha Franklin. We were privy to the intimate celebration hosted by Congressman Benny Hill, and held coveted VIP tickets to the swearing-in ceremony. An invitation to a party hosted by Susan Rice's neighbor further added to the whirlwind of excitement.

As I departed from the inauguration, a newfound sense of possibility had taken root within me. My ambitions soared to heights I had never before dared to imagine. The tireless work I had put in suddenly seemed to demand more—more compensation, more responsibility, more fulfillment. The experience had ignited a hunger in me, a desire to push beyond the limits of what I had previously thought possible for myself. It was a transformative moment, one that would forever alter the trajectory of my life.

6

OPA-LOCKA, FLORIDA

IN 2010, I TOOK A JOB as the Planning and Community Development Director for the City of Opa-locka, a small suburban city in Miami-Dade County, Florida. I was hired by the City Manager at the time, Clarence Patterson. The position came with a considerable salary increase from $77,000 to $132,000 annually—enough to entice me to leave a wonderful, supportive community in Albany, Georgia. Taking this job would expose me to challenges in local government management that I had never encountered before.

My role was to oversee the city's planning, zoning, code enforcement, and economic development functions. It was a diverse community, with a majority Black population but also significant numbers of Hispanic and Caribbean residents. I took pride in working to improve housing conditions, attract new businesses and investments, and enhance quality of life for Opa-locka's citizens.

However, within a year, city commission cuts had stripped away significant portions of my salary package, including a 10 percent pay reduction, a $600 monthly car allowance, and free healthcare benefits for my family—totaling an unexpected loss of about $30,000. The economic instability of the city mirrored the lingering national recession that was caused by the subprime mortgage crisis and excessive risk-taking by banks. In accepting the position in Opa-locka purely out of monetary necessity, I learned a harsh lesson about the volatility of financial incentives.

From the very first commission meeting I attended after being hired, the dysfunction and lack of governance knowledge (or respect for governance) among the elected officials became apparent. Commission members who didn't understand the parameters of the hiring freeze that had been in place questioned why I was hired, unaware that the freeze didn't apply to my position. One commissioner even put forward an agenda item to either approve my hire or send me away, leaving me shaken at potentially being dismissed for no valid reason on my very first day.

This pattern of elected officials overstepping their authority and lacking understanding of their own policies and procedures continued throughout my tenure. Agenda items would be introduced advocating for expenditures the city had no funds to cover. The commission was fractured to the point that meetings devolved into dysfunctional shouting matches rather than productive deliberations. In truth, the city's administrators had their hands tied because we were stuck with a commission that was erratic and irresponsible. This was made clear to me when the commission approved the purchase of ten command cars when our budget department made clear there wasn't money to pay for them. It was no surprise when years after I'd left, Opa-locka nearly went bankrupt but I was shocked and disappointed when commission members were convicted of corruption.

In my roughly five years in Opa-locka, I worked under four different city managers—a shockingly high turnover rate that spoke to the instability and strife within the municipal leadership ranks.

After the departure of Clarence, the city hired Bob Frank, a complete outsider who had never worked in any city manager's office previously. Once, without any investigation, Frank suspended me for five days based on an outrageous claim from a single commissioner that I had lied to the commission—an accusation for which no evidence existed. Though I was eventually reinstated after a former elected official intervened, the incident spoke to Frank's propensity to cave to the commission's most ignorant political winds rather than upholding fair procedures and processes.

Ultimately, Frank's failings led to his termination and the hire of Klay Baxter, someone I actually respected as an innovative manager focused on integrating technology and modern practices.

Unfortunately, Baxter's efforts at reform undertook an embarrassing form when he required every single department head to reapply and re-interview for their own jobs after years of service. I found out about this process not directly from Baxter, but from other planning directors around South Florida calling me to ask if I had been demoted to an assistant role based on the reposting of my position.

In the end, three directors were terminated through Baxter's reapplication process. I kept my role and even took on assistant city manager duties when that position became vacant due to the former assistant's ill health. The revolving door of leadership, scapegoating of staff, and the commission's meddling in daily operations through punitive terminations became all too common during this era.

In 2014, the assistant city manager had to take a leave of absence after a medical occurrence. During his months-long recovery period, I was asked to step in as the acting assistant city manager. Unbeknownst to me at the time, accepting this interim advancement would later prove to be a pyrrhic victory, as it inadvertently set the stage for an unjustifiable blemish on my professional reputation.

In this role, I was responsible for executing the directives of the city manager, mayor, and commission, managing a municipal organization with a $13 million annual operating budget and a workforce of 190 employees, all while serving a population of 16,000 residents. It was a complex and demanding role, but I was determined to rise to the challenge.

One of my first priorities was to address the budget deficit in the Building Services Division. I conducted a thorough analysis of the division's operations and identified areas where we could streamline processes and reduce costs. Through a comprehensive reorganization, we managed to reduce the budget deficit by an impressive 25 percent. Additionally, I spearheaded the creation of the city's first Certificate of Use program, which generated approximately $1 million per annum in revenue. This program not only boosted the city's financial stability but also ensured that businesses were operating in compliance with local regulations.

One of the most critical aspects of my job was directly supervising and managing various departments, including police, human resources, IT, finance, and public works among several others. Each department had its own unique set of challenges and requirements, and it was my responsibility to ensure that they were all functioning efficiently and effectively. I worked closely with department heads to set goals, allocate resources, and monitor progress.

Not long after I departed for my next role in Muskogee, Oklahoma, Baxter also left Opa-locka. An interim city manager was appointed in his place, but this triggered a downward spiral that led to a state of financial emergency being declared in the city.

This interim manager, who I will not name, engaged in egregious pay-to-play corruption. He was found to have extorted a local business owner seeking to open a recycling plant, forcing them to pay kickbacks in exchange for the required city licenses and approvals. The FBI got involved after the business owner wore a wire, leading to the indictments of the city manager, two city commissioners, and a local lobbyist who were all taking bribes in this scheme.

The fallout saw one of the indicted commissioners commit suicide before having to report to prison on the charges. The business owner's own son had also committed suicide years earlier after the struggling recycling facility was being blocked over the bribes—a tragic consequence of the municipal corruption.

Though I had no involvement whatsoever in the federal corruption cases that led to indictments and even suicide by former Opa-locka officials, years later I experience how even a tangential association with a corrupt organization can be used against you.

My experience in Opa-locka was a harsh awakening to the peculiar difficulties of municipal management that diverge sharply from the private sector or even other levels of public administration. In business, you have control over who you hire and can demand professional competence from your team. In local government, you are beholden to the political winds of elected bodies who may value loyalty and patronage over sound management.

Municipal governments are also constrained by a tangle of bureaucratic rules, labor agreements, public meeting laws, and contradicting judicial rulings that handcuff the ability to nimbly adapt and enact reforms. Even as the unelected manager is intended to provide nonpartisan expertise, the overtly partisan elected officials they serve can subvert those efforts through political motivations and blind obstructionism.

It requires a truly unique blend of financial management, policy implementation, public communication, and strategic vision to succeed in local government—all while having to cater to the demands and second-guessing of elected amateurs and make divisive decisions that won't please all constituents. There is no insulation from politics or influence peddling when your nominally impartial role actually requires executing the agenda of partisan leadership.

Nonetheless, I maintain that local government administration is a vital calling that allows dedicated professionals to directly improve the lives of residents through essential public services. Effective municipal managers are truly unsung heroes who grind through the morass of bureaucracy and political headwinds to keep towns and cities operating. My time in Opa-locka bruised my enthusiasm for the field, but also impressed upon me the critical importance of principled, ethical leadership at these local levels of governance.

My cautionary tale should emphasize to others the importance of carefully examining the existing leadership and political cultures of any municipality before taking a management role. Had I done more due diligence on the fractured Opa-locka city commission and its pattern of meddling in staff affairs, I may have foreseen the turmoil to come. But the lure of the short-term financial benefit blinded me to the long-term risks of affiliating with a dysfunctional government. It's a harsh lesson, but one I've learned—prioritize working environments with accountable and ethical leaders who will allow professional management to thrive. In local government, that may be the paramount criteria for pursuing any new opportunity.

One of the few bright spots of my time in Opa-locka was Peggy Castano, who I met just after she'd had her fifth child and was returning to the workforce after focusing on her family. When she came in to interview for the position of my executive assistant, I was immediately impressed by her drive and determination.

Peggy told me directly that even though she had been out of the workforce raising her kids, she was confident she would excel in the role. I remember thinking that a woman who could handle five children was surely capable of handling the demands of the job. Something about her energy and attitude convinced me to take a chance on her.

From her very first day, Peggy proved my instincts right. She was one of the hardest working individuals I've ever encountered. Despite having a large family to care for, she never missed work, never made excuses, and always went above and beyond. I recall one night when we were up against a tight grant deadline, scrambling to get the application in. It was the kind of high-pressure situation where you find out who is really dedicated. While Peggy could have gone home to her family at 5 p.m., she insisted on staying until we got the grant out the door around 11 p.m. She wasn't going to leave us high and dry.

Beyond her work ethic, what really stood out about Peggy was her ambition to keep learning and advancing. At my encouragement, she started taking advantage of the city's tuition reimbursement program by taking classes at Florida Atlantic University. Incredibly, while working full-time and raising five kids, Peggy earned not just her bachelor's degree but a master's as well.

Peggy's talents didn't go unnoticed by others. After I moved on to another position, I got a call from the new city manager of Opa-locka. He told me he wanted to promote Peggy to be his executive assistant and asked if I had any reservations. I told him unequivocally that Peggy was an excellent choice who would serve him well. And that's exactly what she did.

But Peggy's story didn't stop there. Her next boss, the city manager who had promoted her to his assistant in Opa-locka, ended up bringing her along with him to his next job in the city of Lauderdale Lakes. There, he promoted Peggy again, this time to be the Director of Administrative Services.

Peggy's story is one I love to tell—the story of a dedicated public servant who joined my team in an entry-level support position and through talent and tenacity kept rising and rising to the highest levels of municipal management. Peggy's journey from executive assistant to city manager is one of the most impressive and inspiring I've witnessed in my career, and I'm so proud to have played a small part in it by taking a chance on her when she first returned to the workforce. Her success affirms my deep belief in hiring people with potential and then giving them opportunities to grow and advance.

7

MUSKOGEE, OKLAHOMA

WHILE THE DEMISE of my marriage was the spark that rekindled my professional ambitions, the upheaval in Opa-locka fueled those embers into a blazing inferno, launching me toward uncharted territory—straight into the unknown heart of Muskogee, Oklahoma. I'd never set foot in that state before, but stepping off the plane, I felt a curious sense of possibility whispering through the windswept plains.

The interview panel in Muskogee consisted of eight white council members and one Black member. The racial composition was stark, and though I generally shy from making race the focal point, here it mattered. Throughout the town during my visit, I didn't encounter any other Black people. Yet, despite this apparent homogeneity, the community welcomed me with open arms, appointing me their first Black city manager—a testament to their extraordinary character.

It turned out my first impressions were deceptive. There actually was a strong, thriving Black community in Muskogee. As I settled into my new role, invitations to speak at their local churches became a regular part of my weekends, a series I styled as the "Black church speaker circuit." These gatherings allowed me to meet with esteemed preachers and immerse myself in community activities, connecting deeply with the congregation members. This backdrop of acceptance became even more poignant when tragedy struck later on.

When I took over as the new city manager of Muskogee, Oklahoma, I inherited a senior leadership team of thirteen department heads who had all been hired by my predecessor. The previous city manager, who had just retired after an extraordinarily long tenure of thirty-two years, had put his stamp on virtually the entire organizational structure over the course of his three decades in that role.

Despite a prevailing perception that he had run the city operations with an authoritarian "iron fist," it didn't take long for me to identify some glaring structural inefficiencies and antiquated policies that needed modernization. One of the most striking deficiencies was the lack of a crucial deputy or assistant city manager position, leaving no second-in-command to provide operational oversight or leadership continuity in the event of my absence, an untenable risk for a municipality of our size.

Another peculiar structural issue I identified was the excessive proliferation of administrative assistants bloating the workforce across nearly every department and level of leadership. It was common practice not just for each departmental director to have their own dedicated administrative aide, but even deputy directors and assistant directors underneath them would also have individual assistants assigned to support their roles. This seemed grossly excessive to me, especially in contrast to my own city manager's office suite, which had minimal staffing of just a receptionist.

To address what I saw as organizational bloat and lack of strategic lean staffing principles, I recommended that the council approve a multiyear reorganization plan. This would involve proactively eliminating certain excess positions, with a key focus on roles that had remained officially vacant due to turnover for years on end. On average, a staggering 30 percent of our authorized headcount allocation across the municipal workforce sat perpetually vacant and unfilled each year.

My restructuring strategy sought to optimize the inefficient system by implementing a phased attrition approach, targeting the elimination of dispensable positions susceptible to elevated attrition rates. The inflated budgeted headcounts would be reduced by not backfilling positions once vacated. Moreover, I suggested downsizing the bloated administrative assistant workforce that had swelled beyond justifiable numbers.

Looking back, I realize that one of my most significant oversights upon assuming the city manager position was not involving the seasoned department heads earlier in the restructuring plan's creation. As a newcomer taking the helm, I should have more actively sought their internal insights, institutional knowledge, and support before finalizing and presenting the reorganization strategy. By not engaging the affected department directors from the beginning, I unnecessarily generated resistance that subsequently required persuasion and negotiation to surmount once the proposal was revealed.

Despite requiring significant political maneuvering on my part, the city council ultimately approved the reorganization proposal following numerous group and individual discussions where I strived to align their unique priorities. Rather than voting on the plan as a whole, the council elected to consider each proposed position creation or elimination through separate votes. This approach allowed members to signal majority support for the new roles I deemed crucial, notwithstanding broader concerns about my insular plan development.

Much to my relief, the council's individual votes passed each of the new positions I had suggested, including a vital economic development director role. Although the process was more tumultuous than necessary due to my stakeholder missteps, Muskogee's elected officials remained united in backing my core reorganization vision. In the years that followed, some of those newly established positions, such as the economic development director, proved pivotal in rejuvenating the city's long-stagnant tax revenue base.

As an outsider hailing from drastically different environments, I had to swiftly acclimate to Muskogee's distinctive local cultural norms and intricate power dynamics. For instance, when I informed the mayor that I had visited Oklahoma City to attempt recruiting an economic development director for Muskogee, he sternly admonished me, stating, "We don't do that out here. We don't poach people."

Having come from the intensely competitive Miami area, I was accustomed to employees frequently departing for other opportunities, whether within the city or across state lines. However, I quickly discovered that actively recruiting talent from other organizations was frowned upon as a matter of local values and professional norms in Oklahoma, which I needed to respect.

The mayor further elaborated that in their conservative culture, employees should be content with their base salaries and not expect excessive benefits or perks. The concept of enhanced compensation packages to attract or retain talent was viewed with disdain. "Your salary should be enough, and you should be happy to have a job," he bluntly informed me. This was yet another cultural shift I had to adjust to, coming from an environment where robust healthcare, retirement, and other benefits were essential components of workforce strategies.

I also had to adapt my understanding of political power dynamics within the council structure itself. While the mayor was my primary supporter who had hired me, there was a council member who wielded considerable informal authority within his specific ward despite not having an official leadership title.

The councilmember and the mayor disliked each other immensely, so I often found myself awkwardly navigating between their feuding factions. At one meeting where I presented the controversial reorganization plan, the councilmember stated: "Mr. Mayor, I don't know much about this plan, and I'm on the fence about it. But one thing I do trust is Mr. Brown here. I don't like you, Mr. Mayor, but we can agree the city manager is doing a good job. For that reason alone, I'll support his proposal."

This interaction illustrated how I had to develop political capital with all the influential council members, not just the mayor who appointed me, in order to advance key initiatives. In any governing body, there are frequently complex webs of interpersonal histories and power relations that exist beyond just the official hierarchies on paper. Learning to deftly navigate those dynamics would prove essential.

Turning my attention to managing my subordinates, I drew upon lessons from past experiences. One of the first things I did when taking over as Muskogee's city manager was to provide a "Memo of Expectations" to set clear standards and protocols for how I expected my department directors to operate. While some perceived it as excessive or even insulting initially, I had seen firsthand how laying out these detailed guidelines upfront could prevent bigger issues and frustrations from bubbling up later.

The two-page memo covered areas like the need for punctual work hours, procedures for communicating any lateness or absences directly to me, requirements for department heads to attend certain meetings themselves rather than just sending subordinate representatives, and more. I knew it might come across as rigid, but having these expectations documented and acknowledged by my leadership team from the outset would establish proper lines of accountability and convey the high degree of professionalism I valued.

For example, one specific policy was: "If an employee is going to be late or miss a meeting for any reason, I ask that they send me a text, email, or some other direct communication prior to that scheduled time—even if it's a last-minute heads-up. I don't care about the medium; I just need to hear it straight from them personally."

While the Memo of Expectations may have come across as heavy-handed to some initially, I made a point to impress upon employees that it was actually a sign of professional respect. Putting clear communication protocols and boundaries on record from the beginning would allow us to operate with the highest degree of accountability and prevent any misunderstandings or slippages down the line. Ambiguity is the enemy of high-performing teams.

I anticipated that some of my directors might be displeased by my approach, but I was unprepared for one attempting to undermine me. An incident occurred in the city where an individual directly involved with public safety failed a drug test and was discovered to have taken a serious narcotic. In the cities where I had previously worked, such behavior warranted immediate termination, so I instructed the HR director to dismiss the employee. She agreed without hesitation. However, later that day, when the person's supervisor learned of my intention, he visited my office and clarified that the department's binding collective bargaining agreement protected the employee from being fired for a first-time drug-related offense. The employee would have the right to arbitration.

Perplexed by this revelation, I reached out to the HR director, relaying the information I had received. To my surprise, she responded, "Oh, I know that. I know that, but I thought you wanted him terminated." I was stunned. In all my years of management, I had never encountered a direct report attempting to undermine me in this manner. Had we proceeded with the termination, it would have been highly embarrassing and potentially disastrous for the beginning of my tenure as city manager.

Months into my tenure, a tragic officer-involved shooting occurred that put my leadership philosophies around transparency and community relations to the test. A white police officer had shot and killed a young Black college student, Terence Walker, in front of a local church.

Before this incident, I had been clashing with the police chief over my push to outfit officers with body-worn cameras as an accountability and evidentiary tool. The police chief resisted, fearing it was an imposition on police affairs from an outsider unfamiliar with the local realities. But I firmly believed cameras would help protect officers from false allegations while giving the public crucial transparency.

In the aftermath of the shooting, I sought guidance from a seasoned city manager in Sanford who had skillfully navigated the community's response following the tragic shooting of Trayvon Martin, a Black teenager, by George Zimmerman. My colleague emphasized the crucial role of transparency in crisis communication. Armed with his valuable insights and bolstered by the community's confidence in my leadership, the police chief and I took decisive action to release the bodycam footage without delay. This timely response proved instrumental in maintaining the public's trust during this challenging period.

The day before my scheduled evaluation by the city council, I met with the local NAACP and pastors to review the footage frame-by-frame. It clearly showed the student had discharged a firearm after fleeing the officer's attempted questioning, a serious threat that justified the use of force.

While the video details were cut-and-dry, I knew releasing the footage proactively alongside intensive community outreach could help heal racial tensions that had been inflamed by the initial news reports. As anticipated, the NAACP leaders acknowledged they were reassured after seeing how the bodycam exonerated the officer's actions under the circumstances.

So when over 500 vocal Black protesters showed up at my council evaluation the next day, it wasn't out of anger over the shooting itself, thanks to our transparency and engagement efforts. Rather, they had caught wind of council rumors that some members were supposedly going to try terminating me over fallout from the reorganization plan.

The protesters' robust presence in support of my leadership likely dissuaded any anti-incumbent disruptions during my review. While I received some criticism over change management processes from a couple of council members, I was ultimately renewed with a fresh contract and able to keep implementing my key initiatives like the critical economic development role.

This is when I knew for sure that crisis management isn't about calling in fixers like they do on TV dramas; it's about the slow, steady work of building relationships long before disaster strikes.

Ultimately, my experience serving as city manager of Muskogee, Oklahoma, was a deeply challenging yet immensely rewarding crucible that tested my capacities for adaptability, political deftness, cultural integration, and crisis leadership in ways I never could have anticipated. While intensely demanding, it forged invaluable growth, relationships, and hard-won wisdom that have continued to pay dividends in all my executive roles since. I'll forever be grateful for the opportunity to serve the remarkable community of Muskogee and for the indelible lessons that shaped my leadership journey.

8

BELL, CALIFORNIA

MY PATH TO BECOMING city manager of Bell, California, began serendipitously on a plane ride to an ICMA conference in Kansas City. I struck up a conversation with a man who owned a recruitment firm specializing in placing municipal government leaders. When I mentioned my long-standing dream of working in California due to its innovative spirit, Bob said he would keep me in mind if any promising opportunities arose out West. True to his word, Bob called a few months later about an opening for city manager in Bell, a small suburb just southeast of Los Angeles.

I immediately flew out for interviews, somewhat naively booking a hotel room that turned out to be an hour-long drive away from Bell in Rancho Cucamonga. Lesson learned—when interviewing for a city job, always reserve lodging as close to that municipality as possible! I ended up having two rounds of interviews, first with a panel of city managers from neighboring towns and then with the Bell City Council itself. Despite the lengthy trek from my distant accommodations, I must have made a strongly positive impression. The council took a unanimous vote to hire me as Bell's next city manager, making me the first Black individual to hold that position.

Bell had recently been embroiled in a major corruption scandal that dominated national headlines. Several top city officials, including the former mayor and city administrator, had been convicted on charges related to misappropriation of public funds and other financial improprieties. The malfeasance was so severe that the city's bond ratings were downgraded to junk status, severely damaging Bell's reputation and ability to secure favorable borrowing rates.

Upon arriving in Bell, I found a city still sensitive to the misdeeds of the previous administration. When their last permanent city manager left, in a strange quirk, the city charter designated the mayor as the acting city manager. However, the mayor was refusing to sign any documents or payments, likely to avoid being associated with the lingering stench of scandal. As a result, massive backlogs of paperwork had accumulated on the new city manager's desk. I spent my first weeks on the job working thirteen-hour days to vet and process mountains of unsigned contracts, invoices, and other critical documents.

The scandal had also gutted Bell's executive leadership ranks, with many department heads resigning in the aftermath. One of my first priorities was to rebuild a high-functioning management team. I recruited an experienced finance director named Tanya Norton to help prepare my inaugural budget. Tanya, a straight-shooting Asian American woman, came highly recommended based on her strong performances in the neighboring cities of San Gabriel and Long Beach.

When I presented our draft budget at my first council meeting, one of the members, a small business owner, began aggressively interrogating me over various line items. He seemed to be applying a very fiscally conservative private sector lens to municipal finances in a way that revealed some blind spots around standard governmental accounting and procurement practices.

At one point, he asked to hear from the finance director directly. Tanya had no problem with this. In fact, she was able to say what she'd been itching to as the grilling intensified, declaring, "Your city manager is a good manager. He's already explained this, and he knows what he's doing!" Her blunt advocacy shocked the room but exemplified the direct communication style I would come to recognize and appreciate in Tanya. It certainly marked a stark contrast from the more refined, genteel political speech I was accustomed to in my previous roles across the American South. I came to rely on her during my time in Bell.

Restoring community trust in the wake of the scandal was one of my central missions and that of the elected officials in Bell. To that end, we worked diligently to settle a huge backlog of lawsuits and legal claims against the city, eventually winnowing down hundreds of cases to just a handful of holdouts. I collaborated with our finance team to refinance some of Bell's bond obligations to complete construction on a much-needed youth sports complex. Not only did this shore up the city's balance sheet, but it provided a tangible symbol to residents that a new Bell was rising up to invest in future generations.

We also took proactive steps to increase transparency and accessibility to city government. I instituted video recordings of meetings that could be posted online, including an annual State of the City address recapping progress over the prior year. My team expanded our social media presence to better communicate key initiatives, events, and volunteer opportunities.

Not everyone on the council was equally enthusiastic about this new ethos of openness. I remember one member who would often privately float various policy ideas to me then pressure me to present them publicly without attributing their origin. It felt like an attempt to distance themselves from any potential backlash to their own suggestions, but I refused to engage in such political misdirection even if they did have the power to fire me.

After a couple of years in Bell, I gained a greater appreciation for how a relatively small group of highly engaged citizen advocates can affect municipal policymaking. I came to refer to these activists as "crusaders" for their uncanny ability to rally around civic issues and influence council deliberations through persistent public commenting, relationship-building with elected officials and staff, and knack for shaping and reflecting broader community sentiments. The sway of their voices could either reinforce or hinder my administration's policy objectives, but their input unquestionably carried real weight, especially in situations where the wider population remained more apathetic or divided.

One vivid example of the crusaders' power occurred when Bell was considering whether to authorize cannabis dispensaries in the city following California's statewide legalization of recreational marijuana. The city had previously banned medical dispensaries under pressure from a sizeable Lebanese Muslim community that opposed any marijuana businesses on moral grounds. As the council weighed potentially permitting new recreational dispensaries, a huge crowd of residents packed the council chambers to speak against the proposal during public comment.

Many of the speakers belonged to the ethnic and religious groups that had historically held sway over Bell's marijuana policies. In the face of such lopsided opposition, the council members completely reversed course from their initial inclination to approve the dispensaries. They hastily tabled the agenda item and instead directed me to gather more research on potential regulations, essentially punting the vote indefinitely.

This is not to say that elected officials won't stand up to citizen backlash when they believe they are doing what is in the best interest of the city. In the city I led after leaving Bell, I witnessed councils stand resolutely behind contentious decisions in the face of fierce public outcry, when impassioned rhetoric collides with dispassionate data. In Indiantown, Florida, we were exploring whether to establish a municipal fire department or continue contracting those services from the county at exorbitant rates. A consultant's report had indicated that Indiantown could realize substantial savings by creating its own fire district. However, the proposal provoked bitter backlash, particularly among the retiree community, who feared that a town-run department would diminish the quality and responsiveness of emergency services compared to the county's offerings.

We had multiple council meetings where hundreds of seniors showed up to forcefully oppose the fire department plan during public comment. Keep in mind that a typical Indiantown council session might draw a few dozen attendees on a good day, so this was a remarkable demonstration of civic activation. The speakers made impassioned pleas for the council to abandon the proposal, conjuring up nightmare scenarios of people dying from heart attacks or fires burning out of control due to inadequate municipal resources or personnel.

However, in this case, the council members held firm in the face of withering criticism. While acknowledging the sincerity and validity of residents' concerns, they insisted that the consultant's analysis provided a factual basis to move forward with confidence. Weighing the town's precarious finances, the council determined that the potential cost savings of operating an independent fire service outweighed the fear-based objections, as emotionally compelling as those public comments rang in the moment.

In the end, Indiantown successfully launched its own fire department and reaped significant budget savings as a result, vindicating the council's resolve on a contentious issue. The whole episode illustrated that elected officials must sometimes tune out the angry chorus of a fired-up crowd in favor of the math and cold hard numbers. Relying on misleading anecdotes or the passions of a vocal minority can lead cities into disaster, no matter how loud they yell at public meetings.

So in my view, effectively channeling the energy and insights of these civic crusaders remains one of the most challenging balancing acts for any municipal leader. Actively engaging and incorporating the perspectives of mobilized residents is vital for representative democracy to function properly at the local level, where policy choices directly impact people's daily lives. At the same time, professional public administrators must provide their own expertise and recommendations to elected officials based on facts, data, and best practices, even when those conclusions clash with the prevailing political winds. Responsibly reconciling the will of the people with the technical realities of effective governance is the perennial needle that city managers must thread.

Fortunately, my fluency in Spanish, a skill I had developed over many years of study and practice, proved invaluable in building trust and rapport with Bell's predominantly Latino population. I first began learning the language back in high school, continuing on through my undergraduate studies. I came close to attaining a Spanish minor but ended up a few credits shy after opting for an internship experience over a final advanced literature course. Still, I kept up my proficiency by frequently visiting my younger brother, an enlisted sailor, during his naval deployments to Puerto Rico.

By the time I arrived in Bell, I considered myself a fairly confident Spanish speaker, even if I lacked native-level mastery of the language. Unbeknownst to me, however, the staff had made an assumption during the interview process that I did not understand Spanish based on my background. Imagine their shock during my first week on the job when I poked my head out of my office to correct some misinformation I overheard circulating in an impromptu all-Spanish meeting!

From that point forward, word quickly spread among the city employees that their new boss was full of surprises. Whereas prior city managers had struggled to connect with frontline workers, many of whom were first-generation immigrants from Mexico or Central America, I could communicate with them directly in their preferred language. I still remember the looks of happiness and relief on some of their faces when they realized that they could raise concerns or give input without the need for a translator.

My bilingual abilities also opened doors for me to immerse myself in Bell's cultural fabric beyond the confines of City Hall. I was also able to interface more seamlessly with the city's Spanish-speaking business community, many of whom had felt underserved or ignored by municipal programs and economic development initiatives in the past. By meeting with entrepreneurs and shopkeepers in their own language, I gained valuable insights into the unique challenges facing Bell's commercial corridors, from infrastructure needs to public safety concerns.

We were then able to use that feedback loop to better tailor our small business assistance and corridor revitalization efforts.

Ironically, the same linguistic versatility that allowed me to establish credibility quickly with front-line staff and community groups had the opposite initial impact on some members of the city council. A few of the elected officials seemed vaguely unnerved by my ability to build independent relationships with various constituencies whose electoral support they had long taken for granted. I suspect they feared that I might leverage those connections to circumvent their authority or advance my own agenda at their expense.

I was also mindful to reach out to the much smaller but vocal Lebanese Muslim community, who welcomed me into their homes for traditional observances like the post-Ramadan feast of Eid al-Fitr. The local Lebanese bakery even took to surprising me with custom baklava variations, jokingly (or perhaps half-seriously) competing to become the "official" baklava supplier for the city manager's office.

Over time, however, even my most ambivalent council colleagues came to appreciate the advantages of having a city manager who could move fluidly across cultural and linguistic boundaries to keep tabs on the real pulse of the town. They gradually accepted that I had no interest in running for office myself or overshadowing their own political brands. My consistent efforts to loop them in on key discussions with neighborhood and business leaders also helped allay any lingering mistrust about misusing my community access.

Unexpectedly, Los Angeles would become the unlikely backdrop for some of the most profound and meaningful connections of my life. Even though Muskogee had only been a day's drive from all the other places I'd called home, my friends and family found themselves inexplicably drawn to visit me in the City of Angels, where I had settled into a new, amenity-rich apartment in the heart of downtown. It was during one of these visits that my son Clint, who had just completed his fourth year at Florida A&M University, began to confide in me about his struggles in school. Gradually, he revealed that he had fallen behind and feared he might not be able to return.

His words transported me back to my own crossroads moment. Though my circumstances were different, not tied to academic performance, I could have easily found myself in the same predicament, climbing into Jason's car and retreating back home. But Mark had pulled me out of that abyss, and now, I found myself in a position to do the same for Clint.

My first instinct was to reach out to a friend who had once served on FAMU's board of trustees. A few phone calls later, I was connected with an administrator at the school who shed light on Clint's situation. It turned out that while completing the Civil Engineering program might have been an uphill battle, a change in major to mathematics would put him back on track, requiring only a semester or two to wrap up his degree.

Looking back, I can't help but reflect on the invisible threads that bind us to our destiny. Had Clint not finished college, his entire life trajectory would have veered off course. The college-educated woman he would one day marry might never have crossed his path. They would have orbited in different worlds, his academic dreams reduced to a distant "what if."

But I had the means and the knowledge to keep him focused, to guide him over this hurdle. I understood the isolation of being a young person at a crossroads, with no one in your corner to light the way. Our friendship circles, after all, exert a gravitational pull that can rival even the most well-intentioned family members. In those impressionable late teenage years, it's often our peers who shape our decisions and mold our futures.

I knew that if I didn't step in, if I didn't do everything in my power, Clint could easily become another statistic, another promising student who entered college but never emerged with a degree. When he originally asked me to buy him a one-way ticket, he reasoned that he planned to stay the entire summer, I acquiesced. "That makes sense," I told him, not yet realizing that Clint had no intention of returning.

But fate had other plans. With a few semesters of mathematics under his belt, Clint marched across that stage the following year, diploma in hand. It was a narrow escape, a testament to the power of timely intervention and unwavering support. And as I watched him, beaming with pride, I couldn't help but think back to that pivotal moment when I reached out to the board of trustees, setting in motion a chain of events that would alter the course of my son's life forever.

Instead of falling by the wayside, Clint defied expectations. He not only graduated from Florida A&M University but also launched a career in banking and pledged the graduate chapter of my very own fraternity, Omega Psi Phi, but not before pranking his dad.

Growing up, Clint was perpetually surrounded by my fraternity brothers. Through this exposure, he undoubtedly gained a deep understanding and appreciation for the brotherhood of Omega Psi Phi. Yet, he never outwardly expressed any desire to join our ranks. He never tried to do any of our step routines as so many young boys do and there were no casual mentions of wanting to pledge once he reached college.

So, when I received a text message from Clint requesting a serious conversation and found an intake form for another prominent Black Greek-letter organization, Kappa Alpha Psi, attached to it, I was utterly blindsided. Knowing my son as well as I did, he was undoubtedly aware that this revelation would ignite a firestorm of emotions within me.

I immediately dialed his number, my fingers trembling with a mixture of anger and confusion. When he failed to answer, I unleashed a blistering tirade into his voicemail, my voice reverberating with the intensity of my feelings. As I navigated the morning commute, I could feel my blood pressure skyrocketing, the veins in my temples throbbing with each passing mile. Unable to concentrate on the road ahead, I had no choice but to exit the freeway and return home, my mind consumed by this unexpected turn of events.

It was only later that I discovered the truth behind Clint's message. The intake form for Kappa Alpha Psi was nothing more than an elaborate ruse, a prank designed to rattle me to my core. In reality, Clint had already pledged Omega Psi Phi, a fact that filled me with an overwhelming sense of pride and gratitude. The knowledge that my son had chosen to walk the same path I had, to become not just my flesh and blood but my fraternity brother as well, was a gift beyond measure.

I share this story and so much about my background and my family for two reasons. First, I want to demonstrate the importance of having passions outside of work. I also want to demonstrate how we bring our personal lives with us, for better or worse, to the office. I'm not a robot. I don't leave cares about family or my health at home. I take all that with me to the office. We all do.

As my tenure in Bell progressed, I began to sense shifting winds starting to blow in city politics. Although I don't believe I ever fully lost majority support on the council, the margin felt like it was narrowing uncomfortably. A key turning point came when one of my reliable allies casually mentioned that he would be fine with whatever decision the rest of council made about my continued employment, should the matter come up for discussion.

Hearing this conjured thoughts of Tom and his advice to know when to start dusting off the resume. Alarm bells started going off in my head that it might be wise to start contemplating an exit strategy before getting unceremoniously pushed out.

But it was Errin who truly anchored my soul. Our paths had crossed over a decade ago, but it wasn't until I found myself in the sprawling city of Los Angeles that our connection deepened. A trip to Arizona, with its rust-colored canyons and star-filled skies, sealed our fate. Errin possessed a rare kind of magic, an innate ability to draw people in with her warmth and compassion. She was, without a doubt, the most caring and generous woman I had ever encountered. When she accepted my proposal, I felt tremendous joy.

Errin's willingness to join me in Los Angeles was a testament to her love, but I couldn't bear the thought of her sacrificing her thriving pediatric practice in South Florida. She had poured her heart and soul into building a career that allowed her to make a difference in the lives of countless children. As I contemplated my own future, the idea of orchestrating a graceful exit from Bell and California began to take on a new appeal. It offered us the chance to embark on our married life together in South Florida, without the strain of a long-distance relationship stretching across the country. The promise of a new beginning, one that allowed us to nurture our love and build a life together, was too tempting to resist.

I approached the mayor to float the idea of voluntarily transitioning out under agreeable terms. Based on my head-counting, I felt confident that I had at least three solid votes on the council that would approve a severance package, but likely not the unanimous buy-in required to terminate me outright at that moment.

Even though my contract only entitled me to six months of severance, I made the case to the council that paying out the remainder of my term was preferable to keeping me on as a lame duck. I argued that the department heads would start disregarding my authority and direction if they knew my days were definitively numbered. To my great relief, the council agreed with this logic and signed off on my proposed exit deal without forcing a protracted legal battle. It was a valuable lesson that sometimes the most important skill for a city manager is recognizing when it's time to move on gracefully. Extricating myself from Bell with an amicable parting felt like a minor political victory, all things considered.

Looking back on my Bell tenure, the importance of meeting people where they live, in the most literal sense, stands out as an enduring leadership lesson. Breaking down language barriers and participating in cultural rituals demonstrates genuine respect and empathy in a way that no slickly produced government communication campaign can replicate. Even if my Spanish retained a hint of gringo accent, the mere attempt to close the distance spoke volumes to those most often left on the margins of municipal governance.

Of course, none of these successful efforts to steadily rehabilitate a scandal-tarred city would have been possible without a chance encounter on an airplane years earlier. Had I not struck up a random conversa-

tion with the recruiter Bob Murray en route to that fateful ICMA conference, he may have never connected the dots between my aspirations
and the opportunity in Bell. And absent his firm's enterprising associate
recruiter reaching out to me directly, I might have been too preoccupied
with other applications to pursue what seemed like such a daunting political minefield on paper.

But perhaps that's one of the most valuable takeaways from my cir-
cuitous route to Bell: so many pivotal career inflection points hinge on
the capricious currents of sheer luck and casual encounters. You can
sculpt the most impressive resume and rack up a litany of professional
accomplishments, but sometimes the doors of opportunity crack open
through nothing more than a friendly chat with a stranger on a cross-
country flight. Call it coincidence or call it fate, but my California ad-
venture would have never lifted off if I hadn't first taken a chance on
speaking dreams into existence at 30,000 feet.

9

INDIANTOWN, FLORIDA

WHEN I FIRST ARRIVED in the newly incorporated village of Indiantown, Florida, in January 2019 to serve as their inaugural city manager, I knew I was signing up for both an incredible opportunity and immense challenge. Here was a chance to build a brand new municipality quite literally from the ground up—to shape its vision, staff, operations, and trajectory with few constraints. But as the first and only employee initially, I also recognized the myriad hurdles ahead in establishing Indiantown as a thriving, professionally run city ready to handle the explosive population growth already on the horizon.

Indiantown itself has a fascinating history, originally established by Seminole traders back in the early 1900s and later settled by white frontier migrants in the 1890s. The community's development kicked into overdrive in 1924 when businessman S. Davies Warfield constructed a spur of the Seaboard Air Line Railway right through the heart of town. Warfield had grand ambitions to make Indiantown the southern headquarters of his railroad empire. To that end, he plotted out streets, constructed housing, a school, and the stately Seminole Inn that still stands today as a historic landmark.

However, Warfield's grand plans were cut short when the great Florida land boom went bust in 1926. He passed away a year later, and a major 1928 hurricane dealt further blows that halted development for decades, relegating Indiantown to somewhat of a rural backwater—albeit one with good bones for future growth thanks to Warfield's infrastructure investments. That future finally arrived on December 31, 2017, when Indiantown formally incorporated as the 411th municipality in Florida.

When I interviewed for the city manager position in December 2018, a couple of months after leaving my previous role in Bell, I was immediately drawn to the exciting potential for community building in Indiantown. Beyond the professional opportunity, on a personal level the village felt similar to Pensacola where I had deep roots. It was a diverse community with a multicultural village council that appealed to my values. The fact that it was located close to where I was already living sealed the deal.

So in early January 2019, I began my tenure as Indiantown's first-ever permanent city manager with the title Village Manager. Having an urban planning background, I felt well equipped to handle the core challenge of guiding the explosive growth and development already on the horizon. But first, I had to assemble a municipal workforce from thin air. One of my first orders of business was to explain to the village council that we couldn't just rely on temporary contractors to fulfill key staff functions like finance and operations—we needed our own permanent personnel and I would need their support to make those hires.

Over the next three years, I grew Indiantown's staff from a one-man show to a union workforce of 36 full-time employees across all municipal functions. We outsourced a few major services like fire and police to the county, which allowed us to keep our in-house team lean and efficient. But my projections showed we would still need to bring on around

100 additional personnel within the next two years to keep pace with our extraordinary growth rate.

When I first started as manager, Indiantown had a population of about 8,000. But thousands of new housing units had already been approved and were poised to break ground. Practically overnight, we were staring down a tripling of our population to 24,000 residents within a 5-year span. In my mind, building out our staff to provide quality services and infrastructure to match that growth rate was priority number one.

Of course, as the saying goes, the urgent should never supplant the important, and there was perhaps no more important long-term issue facing Indiantown than securing control of our own water and sewer services. When I arrived, the village's utilities were privately owned by an outside provider that was a constant source of resident complaints over poor service and high costs. We had zero leverage over the situation, which is just untenable for any municipality, let alone a fast-growing one.

I made acquiring that water and sewer utility one of my top priorities and was able to negotiate a deal with the owner to purchase the system outright. Even better, because we met all the low-income metrics, I was able to secure a very favorable loan from the state Department of Environmental Protection to finance the acquisition. Thanks to those qualifications, that loan ended up converting to a grant for 80 percent of the total cost. This was one of the largest utility deals done by any municipality with the DEP in Florida at that time. Suddenly, Indiantown had full control over its water and sewer and we were able to make crucial upgrades and provide far better service—all at minimal cost to taxpayers. It was a huge win.

However, not everyone was thrilled with the progress we were making. When Indiantown first incorporated, it was pushed by a group of developers and business interests who had counted on getting their preferred candidates into office to control the agenda. But the actual residents had other ideas and instead voted in a more community-oriented council skeptical of unbridled development.

Almost immediately upon my arrival, a couple of local bloggers closely aligned with the pro-growth crowd began a relentless smear campaign against me and the council majority. These adversaries would accuse me of participating in the widely known corruption, and some even claimed I had been fired despite proof otherwise.

One blogger in particular was especially ruthless, constantly posting articles on Facebook painting me as this corrupt, unqualified charlatan from out of town who was just manipulating the council for my own ends. She hammered the message that I was saddling the village with debt and wasting taxpayer money at every turn. It was all baseless nonsense, but she had a devoted following, especially among an older crowd in a community called Indianwood who seemed to uncritically believe her every word.

In one instance, a public records request turned up no documentation of my interim assistant city manager position, sparking a libelous news report that I had fabricated that role. I had to go to extensive lengths providing documentation to council members to reaffirm the facts. Some went so far as to defame me by claiming I practiced "black supremacy" in my role—an outrageous claim given the majority African American and Hispanic demographics of the city.

Another major critic had a local streaming talk show where he would regularly go on unhinged rants about me and the council. Eric made it sound like I was this criminal mastermind who had looted Opa-Locka before landing in Indiantown to do the same. His attacks were filled with wild misinformation and fabrications, but he had a platform and an audience who ate it up.

Things got so bad that residents would angrily confront me in public, parroting the bloggers' false claims that I was corrupt and unfit for office. They would say I had this baggage and shady past, that I was under FBI investigation, you name it. It was like arguing with a brick wall—no amount of facts could overcome the fiction they had bought into. As a city manager, you're not in a political role, so you can't really push back forcefully without escalating the situation. I just had to grin and bear it while focusing on doing my job.

In reality, the Opa-Locka scandal (which was very real) involved crimes committed by my successor and other officials after my tenure. I had absolutely zero involvement and there was not a shred of evidence connecting me to their schemes. But that didn't stop this blogger from constantly insinuating otherwise. It felt like a bad dream getting ambushed in the final stages of interviews with printed-out copies of these scurrilous hit pieces. Even when I would present the clear facts and obvious timeline proving the allegations false, the mere presence of the smears often can plant fatal doubts in the minds of hiring committees.

For a public servant, there's little recourse in fighting this kind of defamation. The bar for proving libel is extremely high for public figures and requires demonstrating a direct line between the lies and tangible damages. Without documented proof that I was passed over for specific jobs exclusively due to the smears, any legal action would be an expensive and likely doomed effort. It was a brutal and demoralizing position—watching a faceless blogger hiding behind anonymity single-handedly try to sabotage my once-sterling professional reputation without consequence.

At times, it felt like an existential crisis. I had dedicated my entire adult life to integrity and excellence in municipal government—building strong communities, sound budgets and effective workforces that uplifted people's quality of life. Now, a complete fiction promulgated by bloggers that would get laughed out of a fact-checking process was torpedoing my prospects and erasing decades of tireless work. I was collateral damage in a cowardly political hit job, with painfully few options to fight back.

I ultimately resolved to focus my energy where I actually had agency. I put my head down and kept doing the hard work of city management—building trust with residents face-to-face, delivering on promises and proving my worth through action, not words. People who knew me and saw the fruits of my labor understood the attacks were bogus. In time, I began to secure new opportunities based on the merits and my personal relationships, circumventing the noise. It's still ongoing, but I've made peace with the reality that all I can control is showing up with integrity and results every day.

A major challenge I faced at Indiantown came during the COVID-19 crisis right as the pandemic hit. Like many conservative areas, our residents were extremely skeptical of both the virus' severity and of the government's role in the public health response. Many openly questioned whether the coronavirus was even real as the outbreak spiraled.

To make matters worse, the county health department was dragging its feet in supporting our efforts. Indiantown had a large immigrant population, with around 70 percent being Guatemalan American. The majority were primarily Spanish-speaking, but most spoke one of three indigenous Central American dialects called K'iche', Mam, and Kaqchikel in their daily lives. I tried communicating to the authorities that we desperately needed public health information and outreach in those languages, not just Spanish, but it fell on deaf ears. They didn't want to spend the money.

So we were left to confront a severe viral threat with widespread skepticism from residents and limited support from the county. As cases began to mount, I lobbied for a mask mandate in our municipality, which my council supported. But because Indiantown was a recently incorporated town, we didn't have our own police force yet and were reliant on the county sheriff for enforcement. Well, the sheriff himself was elected and cognizant of the political winds, so he flat-out refused to enforce our mask ordinance, which severely undercut its effectiveness.

My last recourse was the bully pulpit, trying to persuade our community to take the situation seriously and abide by our regulations. But it was an uphill battle. Large churches would still hold unmasked gatherings with thousands in attendance, creating superspreader events that radiated through our neighborhoods. When I got word of one revival meeting poised to host over 1,000 parishioners without masks, I personally went down to the church and served them with a cease-and-desist order. Thankfully, the organizers complied and shut it down without further incident, but it underscored how much rested on voluntary adherence.

In the end, Indiantown was one of the hardest-hit regions in a state that already had a high rate of COVID deaths. Our residents were already at high risk, with extremely high rates of obesity and chronic illnesses. Coupled with the slower response, it was a recipe for disaster. I truly believe that if the situation had been taken more seriously from the jump—communicating clearly in the right languages and backing up our efforts—we would have had a better outcome.

The experience was eye-opening for me in illuminating the power of disinformation to warp public perceptions and collective action—often with deadly results. I saw firsthand how deeply ingrained mistrust of government within certain ideological cultures can become a vector for a pandemic's spread. In times of crisis, the only antidote is having already established deep reserves of trust and open lines of engagement across community stakeholders. Building those dynamics can't happen on the fly—it requires long-term commitments and proactive outreach during calmer periods. It's a lesson I've carried into all my subsequent roles.

As I reflect back on these pivotal episodes in my city management career, I'm struck by the common threads. Whether shepherding the growth of newly incorporated municipalities, battling coordinated smear campaigns, or mounting pandemic responses, the core determinant of positive outcomes always comes back to trust. Trust is the reservoir of goodwill that allows progress to be made even in the face of vehement opposition. Trust is what inoculates communities against the viral spread of disinformation. And trust is ultimately what allows public servants like myself to keep going in the face of daunting headwinds and bad-faith attacks on our integrity.

Building that trust is a painstaking endeavor that happens in a million tiny interactions over many years. It's showing up authentically and consistently for the residents in both their proudest and most challenging moments. It's bringing creativity and determination to thorny municipal problems and delivering solutions that actually move the needle on people's lives. And most importantly, it's keeping your head up and staying true to your principles even when the slings and arrows are flying from all directions.

While the experiences I've shared here rank among the greatest trials of my professional life, they also reaffirmed my resolve in this work. The public depends on dedicated institutions and tireless civil servants to be the steady hand on the tiller guiding their communities, often through uncharted waters. We won't always get it right, and the temptation to quit in the face of withering headwinds can be immense. But we owe it to our neighbors and cities to answer the call of service with everything we can muster.

For a while there, my efforts spoke for themselves. Despite the non-stop online attacks, by 2021 the fruits of our labor were impossible to ignore. Roads were being paved, new infrastructure was getting built, beautification projects were raising property values and Indiantown was indisputably on the rise. That election cycle, the two council members up for reelection who had supported my agenda won handily as residents saw the positive changes firsthand.

But the opposition didn't relent. They just shifted their message from targeting me to claiming the council majority were "obstruction-ists" holding back the rightful pro-development agenda. Lo and behold, in 2023 they eked out razor-thin victories, unseating two of my three main council allies—one of them by a mere six votes. The winds had shifted.

One of the newly elected members, a former sheriff's deputy, imme-diately began making wildly false accusations against me, claiming I had mismanaged funds and done all sorts of unethical things. He never once even tried to meet with me or learn the facts, he just regurgitated base-less rumors as truth. It was obvious this new majority's real goal was to force me out and install a manager who would do the development industry's bidding.

I often tell young people considering a career in local government that this work is not for the thin-skinned or the faint of heart. You will be tested in ways that can shake you to the core. But you'll also have the rare opportunity to touch lives and shape trajectories at a scale that few other professions can match. For those who are ready to plant their feet and fight for their communities, there is no higher calling than public service. The road is long and winding—as I can certainly attest! But the destination is always worth the journey.

After four years of pouring my heart and soul into building Indiantown up from scratch, I wasn't about to let my reputation be dragged through the mud. If they wanted a political hatchet job, they were going to have to do it on someone else's time. So in mid-2023, I negotiated an exit on my own terms. I knew in my heart I had done right by the people of Indiantown and had laid a strong foundation for the future. Walking away was still emotionally wrenching after investing so much of myself in the community, but I left with my head high.

Looking back, I'm immensely proud of what my team and I accomplished in such a short timespan. In four years, we transformed a rural hamlet of 8,000 into a professionally administered, financially sound, rapidly diversifying small city of 24,000. We built an excellent municipal workforce from the ground up, made major infrastructure upgrades, took control of essential services and laid the groundwork for sustainable growth. By the time I left, Indiantown had a $26 million rainy day fund and was well positioned for the future.

10

THE FUTURE

AS I STOOD ON THE sun-drenched shore of Pensacola watching my grandchildren chase seagulls with my dragon kite, I couldn't help but reflect on the journey that had brought me to this moment of tranquility. Thirty years in municipal management had left me as battered and wind-worn as my decades-old kite, but here I was, still aloft, still navigating the ever-shifting currents of public service.

It hadn't been long since I'd returned from Harvard University's certificate program for state and local government executives. Those six weeks had been a whirlwind of intellectual stimulation and practical wisdom, leaving me dizzy with newfound knowledge and perspective. I was still having new revelations remembering the transformative experience.

From the moment I stepped into the hallowed halls of Harvard, I was immersed in an environment of intellectual rigor and practical wisdom. To say the lecture on innovative financing strategies for public projects was informative would be an understatement. As my peers and I delved into case studies from across the nation, I found my preconceptions about municipal funding mechanisms challenged and expanded. The professor, a luminary in the field, guided us through a maze of complex financial instruments, revealing how cities can leverage private-public partnerships and creative bond structures to fund critical infrastructure projects without overburdening taxpayers.

Having just come out of the COVID-19 pandemic, the workshop on crisis communication was truly powerful. We weren't just discussing theory; we were living it. The simulated crisis scenario echoed the experiences I'd just had in real life. And as I crafted public statements, fielded questions from mock reporters, and coordinated with emergency services, I only wished I'd done the program years earlier.

My group's visit to a nearby smart city was a glimpse into the future of urban management. Walking through their state-of-the-art operations center, I saw firsthand how data analytics and technologies could revolutionize everything from traffic management to waste collection. The city's leadership team was refreshingly candid about the challenges they faced in implementation.

What I appreciated most were the connections forged with fellow participants. Late-night discussions in the dorm common rooms became impromptu think tanks, where city managers from across the country shared their triumphs and tribulations. I found myself learning as much from the small-town administrator in the rural Plains as I did from the deputy mayor of a major metropolitan area. These conversations broadened my perspective, challenging me to think beyond the confines of my own city's borders and see the interconnectedness of our urban challenges.

Perhaps the most impactful aspect of the program was the Outward Bound team-building experience. Our first task seemed simple: navigate a series of obstacles as a team. Yet, as we fumbled and faltered, it became clear that our corporate titles and individual achievements meant little here. We were stripped of our usual trappings of authority and forced to rely on each other in ways we never had before.

As we tackled increasingly complex challenges throughout the day, I felt a shift in our group dynamic. The artificial barriers that often exist among high achievers melted away. The comedian in our group emerged as a strategic thinker. The assertive mayor learned the value of stepping back and listening. And I, the self-assured city manager, discovered the humility to ask for help when I needed it.

One particular moment stands out. We were tasked with crossing a simulated ravine using only a few planks and our collective ingenuity. As we debated strategies, tensions rose, and for a moment, it seemed we might fail. But then, something remarkable happened. We stopped talking and started listening—really listening—to each other. Ideas flowed, roles naturally emerged, and before we knew it, we had not only crossed the ravine but had done so with a level of cohesion and mutual support I had rarely experienced in my professional life.

The physical and mental challenges pushed us to our limits, but they also revealed our potential. I watched as colleagues who had been aloof became a unified force, solving problems with creativity and determination. We celebrated each other's strengths and supported each other through moments of vulnerability.

As the day drew to a close, we gathered for a reflection session. The insights shared were profound. We talked about trust, communication, and the power of diverse perspectives. We discussed how the lessons learned on this island could transform our approach to leadership and teamwork back in our local governments.

Then, on the shore of Thompson Island, gazing out at the Boston skyline shimmering across the harbor, I had the first in a series of revelations. The time had come for me to not only lead, but to teach others to lead.

Not long after I returned from Harvard, I attended the first post-pandemic gathering of the International City/County Management Association (ICMA) where a cluster of my former colleagues and I caught up over a leisurely lunch, during which the inevitable question arose: since I'd resigned from Indiantown, Florida, what was I going to do next?

I explained to them that I was going to start a government consulting company. This intrigued them but the big reveal was how invaluable a tool ChatGPT had been in my company formation process. I'll never forget the bemused looks on my colleagues' faces.

My son Clint had been the first to show me ChatGPT. When I first used it, it felt like glimpsing a magic trick. Suddenly, tasks that used to take me hours could be accomplished with a few keystrokes. It had all begun prosaically enough with a simple query to chat: "How do I start a consulting company?" From that humble entry point, our collaboration had blossomed into a fertile creative partnership.

As I explained, one particularly skeptical lunch companion, Tina, remained steadfastly unconvinced of the utility of ChatGPT, so I asked her what office task she was currently working on. A municipal resolution for the city council, as it transpired. I promptly relayed the pertinent details to ChatGPT, and it proceeded to compose a resolution of such stellar quality that even Tina became a believer.

Coincidentally, the afternoon's plenary session concerned this very topic of artificial intelligence. During a moment of participatory spectacle, an auditorium full of suit-clad civic professionals were asked to raise their hands if they had any experience interfacing with chat. Only my small lunch cadre found our hands aloft. It was clear no one in local government understood the implications for the rapid pace of technological change. As someone who had always been an early adopter of technology and marveled at how I'd gone from clunky desktop computer to the sleek device that fit in my pocket. But as I listened to my colleagues trade war stories about botched software rollouts and skeptical staff, I realized that the real challenge wasn't the technology itself, but the mindset shift it required. For a profession steeped in tradition and hierarchy, the idea of entrusting key functions to algorithms and automation was understandably daunting.

As I explored the conference halls and attended session after session, I had another revelation: the future was here. It had snuck up on us like a cotton boll and many of us were scrambling to catch up.

It seemed everywhere I turned, managers were grappling with how to integrate new tools and systems into their operations. There was confusion surrounding everything from AI-powered chatbots to cloud-based collaboration platforms. The pandemic's receding tide left behind a workplace transformed, yet a stubborn contingent clamored for a return to the old ways. Their voices echoed a deeper resistance—a reluctance to embrace the changing face of our workforce, one that was shifting from aging baby boomers to millennials and even Gen Z.

As I listened to apprehensive managers, on a certain level, I could understand their anxiety. The disconnect between our generation and theirs was palpable—their motivations and approaches to work a stark contrast to my own formative years. In my twenties, I had been a paragon of traditional ambition—juggling multiple jobs, supporting a family, all while pursuing a master's degree. Sleep was a luxury, weekends a myth. But this new cohort of millennials seemed to operate on a different frequency.

However, my experience over the years with younger workers has led me to realize that millennials were far from a monolithic group. Take Wes Jenkins, for instance. A millennial with more ink than skin showing, Wes was a rising star I promoted to parks director, much to the chagrin of his former manager. "He lacks the maturity," she had whispered, her concern palpable. But I saw beyond the tattoos to the late nights Wes put in, the passion that radiated from him. My gamble paid off—Wes flourished, his success a rebuke to those who would write off potential based on generational stereotypes.

I concede, however, that everyone is not a Wes. I also had a Steve—the Ivy League wunderkind whose polished pedigree belied a startling lack of practical skills. Steve's tenure as our public information officer was a cautionary tale writ large. Despite his impressive credentials, he floundered with basic tasks. Press releases became exercises in grammatical gymnastics, social media a digital minefield.

The nadir came during a crisis involving a local blogger spreading misinformation about our city council. Instead of confronting the issue head-on, Steven retreated, allowing falsehoods to proliferate unchecked. When called to account, he crumbled, tears flowing as freely as his excuses. The final straw? Steve claiming credit for a major water utility acquisition he'd barely touched, a fabrication that spoke volumes about his character.

Yet, Steve's failings weren't entirely his own. They reflected a broader challenge—how to bridge the gap between academic achievement and real-world competence. It was a reminder that diplomas, while valuable, are no substitute for emotional intelligence and practical experience.

My own children, millennials themselves, have been my personal case studies in this generational evolution. My son, Clint, at thirty, displayed a level of professional maturity I had reached nearly a decade earlier at twenty-two. Yet, his journey was no less valid. Through perseverance and an embrace of new technologies—he introduced me to the wonders of ChatGPT—Clint found his own path to success.

My daughter, Cierra, took a different route entirely. She embraced body art, becoming an entrepreneur in a field that would have been unthinkable in my early career. Both of my children, despite their divergent paths, share a common thread with their peers: a desire for fulfilling, self-directed lifestyles.

Their experiences taught me that empathy and patience were key to developing millennial talent. Just as my mentors had shown forbearance with my youthful naiveté, I learned to provide the same grace period for this new generation to grow—all while maintaining high standards of accountability. The generational divide in our workforce is not a chasm to be feared, but a bridge to be built. It's in the crossing that we'll find the strength, innovation, and resilience to serve our communities in the years to come.

As I navigated these turbulent generational waters, I found myself confronting my own biases. I thought of Louis Diaz, a hire that challenged my preconceptions. Louis, with his long biker hair and Hells

Angels aesthetic, seemed an odd fit for government work. Yet his competence was unquestionable, his work ethic impeccable.

Over time, Louis's Friday office attire became increasingly dramatic—chains, wilder hair, and fingernails that raised eyebrows. But his ability to seamlessly transition from weekend warrior to consummate professional never wavered. Louis was a living reminder that appearance and ability often have little correlation.

I think back to the young man I once was, forced to shed his high-top fade and "diamond" earrings to be taken seriously. I weep for him, for the narrow mindset that equated appearance with competence. Now, I urge my peers to look beyond the surface, to see the potential that lies within each individual, regardless of their generation or style.

The pandemic forced us to confront perhaps the most pressing issue of all—the future of work itself. Remote work, once an exception, became a norm. For a profession steeped in tradition, this shift was seismic. How could we maintain cohesion, gauge morale, foster collaboration when our teams were scattered to the winds?

The answer, I've come to believe, lies in redefining productivity. It's not about hours logged or faces seen, but results achieved. It's about setting clear expectations and trusting our people to meet them, wherever they may be. This new paradigm requires a different kind of leadership—one that values output over optics, that can balance autonomy with accountability.

I mulled over all this as I stood on the beach, watching my grandchildren marvel at the dragon-tailed kite bobbing above the dunes. When I handed the kite string to my grandson, his face lit up as he navigated the wind for the first time.

Just as I was teaching my grandson to fly a kite, I understood the importance of passing on the reins of leadership to the next generation of public servants. It's about creating a culture of continuous learning and development in government offices, one that values experimentation and innovation over blind adherence to the status quo. By entrusting the younger generation with the complex winds of governance, we allow them to bring fresh energy and new perspectives to public service, ensuring its continued relevance and effectiveness.

As the sun dipped towards the horizon, painting the sky in hues of orange and pink, I contemplated the future of public service. The challenges facing our profession are daunting, the winds of change blowing stronger than ever. But we have the tools and the talent to rise to the occasion, to adapt and thrive in this new reality.

In the end, that's what public service is all about—rising to meet the needs of the moment, even when it's hard, even when it's scary. It's about holding fast to our values while embracing the possibilities of the future. It's about learning to dance on the wind, to find joy in the journey, and to lift others up along the way.

As we packed up our kites and headed home, sand between our toes and salt in our hair, I felt a renewed sense of purpose. Looking at my grandchildren, their faces flushed with the excitement of the day, I knew that the future was in good hands.

AFTERWARD

POCKET GUIDE FOR LOCAL GOVERNMENT PROFESSIONALS

As I reflect on my career in local government, I've come to realize there's one thing I wish I had when I first started: a brief primer. This realization has inspired me to create just such a guide for those following in my footsteps.

When I began my journey in public service, I often felt overwhelmed by the unique challenges and complexities of local government. A concise, practical guide would have been invaluable in helping me navigate those early years more effectively. It could have provided a roadmap for understanding the distinct context of local governance, offered strategies for continuous skill development, and given insights into proactive career management within the public sector.

My hope is that this quick guide will serve as a compass for newcomers and seasoned professionals alike. It distills years of experience into essential wisdom, helping readers grasp the nuances of public service more quickly. By offering guidance on maintaining a service-minded approach and balancing the often-challenging work with personal integrity and perseverance, it can help others craft fulfilling and impactful careers in local government.

My hope is that this guide will empower the next generation of public servants to hit the ground running. It's designed to illuminate the path toward strengthening communities and improving lives—the core of what makes a career in local government so uniquely meaningful. By sharing the lessons I've learned, I aim to contribute to the continued excellence and effectiveness of our public institutions, ensuring they remain vibrant and responsive to the needs of our communities.

Introduction: Government vs. Private Sector (Key Differences)

Mission and Objectives

The fundamental objectives and incentives of local government differ significantly from those of the private sector. While private companies are primarily driven by profitability and delivering value to shareholders, government agencies are focused on serving the public interest and providing essential services to citizens.

One key difference lies in the mission and objectives. Government's mission is to serve the public good, promote equity, and ensure access to vital services. This means making decisions and allocating resources in a way that benefits the overall well-being of the community, even if it doesn't necessarily generate revenue. In contrast, the private sector aims to generate profits and grow market share. Businesses make decisions based on what will maximize returns for owners and shareholders.

Funding

Funding is another major distinction. Local governments are funded through taxes, fees, and allocations from federal and state governments. They have to be prudent stewards of public funds and justify their spending to citizens and oversight bodies. Private companies, on the other hand, generate revenue through selling goods and services. They have more flexibility in how they allocate their resources, but are ultimately accountable to their bottom line.

Accountability

This leads to a difference in accountability. Governments are accountable to citizens and elected officials. They are expected to be transparent, respond to public inquiries and complaints, and make decisions that reflect the will of the people they serve. Private companies are primarily answerable to their shareholders and customers. While they may engage in socially responsible practices, their ultimate accountability is to generating returns and satisfying paying clients.

Scope of Services

The scope of services is also much broader in government. Local governments provide a wide array of public services, from education and public safety to infrastructure and social services. They can't easily choose to discontinue or outsource services that are essential to the functioning of a community. Private companies have more flexibility to specialize in specific industries and products/services that are profitable.

Decision-making

Decision-making in government involves weighing many competing interests. Policy decisions have to take into account the needs of different constituencies, the long-term public good, fiscal constraints, legal requirements, and political considerations. It's a complex balancing act. In business, decision-making can be more singularly focused on the bottom line, even if companies still have to navigate regulations and stakeholder concerns.

Public Scrutiny

Finally, the level of public scrutiny is much higher for governments. As entities funded by and serving the public, they are subject to open records laws, media inquiries, and direct input from citizens. Elected officials' communications and personal lives are often subject to examination. While businesses certainly face reputational and regulatory pressures, they generally operate with less transparency and public involvement in their day-to-day affairs.

Understanding these key differences between the public and private sectors is essential for success in a local government career. The skills and mindset needed to thrive are shaped by this unique context. With that foundation, let's explore advice for building an impactful career at different stages.

Government Professionals

Growing up in Pensacola, Florida, I experienced firsthand the challenges that many local government employees face in their early lives. Like so many of my colleagues, I came from a modest background, relying on government assistance programs like food stamps and free school lunches to make ends meet. These experiences instilled in me a deep respect for the vital role that government plays in supporting communities and providing opportunities for those who need them most.

From a young age, my grandmother taught me the value of hard work and dedication. Whether I was helping her clean event halls on weekends or accompanying her on housekeeping jobs, she made it clear that integrity, punctuality, and attention to detail were non-negotiable. These early lessons formed the bedrock of my work ethic and have stayed with me throughout my career in local government.

As I navigated my way through college and graduate school, I encountered countless examples of the commitment and resilience that define public service. From the employment office supervisor who patiently mentored me during a high school internship to the fraternity brothers who modeled academic excellence and community leadership, I was surrounded by individuals who embodied the best of what it means to serve others. I also noticed that my fellow students who were pursuing careers in local government came from a wide range of backgrounds and brought diverse perspectives to our discussions and projects.

In fact, one of the strengths of the local government workforce is its diversity and high level of education compared to the private sector. Many of my colleagues hold advanced degrees in fields like public administration, urban planning, social work, and engineering. This expertise allows us to tackle complex challenges and develop innovative solutions that benefit our communities. Additionally, the diversity of our workforce helps us better understand and serve the needs of the increasingly diverse constituents we represent.

Today, as a local government professional, I see these same qualities reflected in my colleagues every day. We come from diverse backgrounds, but we share a common bond: a deep appreciation for the power of government to make a positive difference in people's lives. Whether we're working to improve public safety, enhance community services, or support economic development, we approach our work with the same dedication, integrity, and respect for the public trust that has been instilled in us from an early age. It is this shared commitment to service, combined with our expertise and diversity, that makes local government such a rewarding and impactful career path.

Early Career Professionals

Starting the Journey

As an aspiring local government professional, my journey began with an internship that I secured through a competitive process at my university. From the outset, I understood the importance of making the most of this opportunity by becoming an expert on the organization, honing my communication skills, and building relationships with colleagues. Following my internship, I was hired in a full-time role where I continued to learn and grow, achieving certifications and demonstrating initiative by developing new programs and pioneering processes.

Overcoming Challenges

Throughout my early career, I faced significant challenges, such as low pay and long hours, which required me to take on additional jobs to support my family. Despite these obstacles, I remained committed to hard work, continuous learning, and enthusiasm for my work in local government. I was fortunate to have mentors whose guidance and support were instrumental in launching my career. To succeed, I soaked up knowledge everywhere I could and asked thoughtful questions.

Finding the Right Role

For those just starting out, local government offers abundant opportunities to quickly gain experience in public service and build important skills. The key is to find the right role, make the most of your early experiences, and set yourself up for future growth. Many entry-level positions don't require extensive specialized expertise, though certain roles may call for specific academic backgrounds like engineering, social work, public health, or urban planning.

Common entry-level opportunities include internships or fellowships, administrative assistant positions, analyst or coordinator roles in departments matching your skillset, and frontline positions interacting directly with the public. To find openings, monitor the websites of jurisdictions that interest you, attend job fairs and professional events, network with local government professionals, and get involved with relevant community organizations.

Understanding the Importance of First Impressions

As a young professional embarking on my career journey, I quickly realized the crucial role that first impressions play in shaping one's path. Drawing from my experiences in short-term jobs and military service, I understood that the level of commitment and performance expected in a professional setting would be significantly higher than in my previous roles.

Researching the Organization

To set myself up for success, I began by researching the organization I was about to join. I relied on my network, including professors and career counselors, to gain valuable insights into the employment landscape. This helped me understand the organization's culture, expectations, and the challenges I might face.

Planning Professional Attire

Next, I turned my attention to selecting the right professional attire. Recognizing that workwear plays a significant role in how one is perceived, I erred on the side of caution and opted for more professional clothing when in doubt. Seeking guidance from my hiring manager proved to be a wise decision, as they provided valuable input on the organization's dress code and expectations.

Crafting a Personal Introduction

Finally, I focused on crafting a personal introduction that would make a positive impression during the onboarding process. I prepared a brief yet engaging summary of my background, education, and hobbies, ensuring that I could connect with my new colleagues on a personal level while showcasing my unique qualities and experiences.

The First 30 Days

Adopting a Service Mindset

I approached my new role with a focus on serving both colleagues and customers. Despite my desperation for a job in my field of study, I was immensely appreciative of this ground-floor opportunity and was determined to make the most of it.

Learning and Observing

The initial month was spent absorbing cultural cues, understanding communication preferences, and identifying key stakeholders and expected behaviors. I had an office where people would come by and ask personal questions, allowing me to establish connections and gain insights into the organization's dynamics.

Setting Expectations with Management

I took the initiative to clarify my role's big-picture objectives and daily expectations, including work hours and meeting attendance. I actively contributed to the development of programs and handled various tasks referred to me by different departments. I worked closely with colleagues to understand and execute my responsibilities effectively.

Engaging with Colleagues

I invested time in understanding my coworkers' roles and how I could add value to their work and the organization. By fostering strong relationships and demonstrating a willingness to collaborate, I positioned myself as a valuable team member.

Seeking and Acting on Feedback

I actively requested feedback from my superiors and colleagues, using it as a tool for continuous improvement and growth. Constructive criticism was crucial in shaping my professional development, and I adapted my approach accordingly.

Establishing SMART Goals

Although I was unaware of the concept at the time, I was effectively setting SMART (Specific, Measurable, Achievable, Relevant, and Time-bound) goals to help me learn and adapt quickly. My first project involved creating a community survey in an area affected by blight, where I developed a ranking system for properties. By utilizing spreadsheet applications, I was able to showcase my skills and present statistical data effectively.

Taking Personal Responsibility for Learning

I took ownership of my professional growth by tracking my weekly progress, reflecting on my strengths, challenges, and areas for improvement. This proactive approach allowed me to identify opportunities for development and seek out the necessary resources to bridge any gaps in my knowledge or skills.

Networking and Building Relationships

I recognized the importance of networking and actively sought to build strong relationships within the organization. By connecting with colleagues across various departments and levels, I gained a deeper understanding of the organization's operations and positioned myself as a collaborative and approachable team member.

The Second 30 Days

Accelerating Learning and Doing

As I entered my second month on the job, I focused on adopting a growth mindset and being proactive in my responsibilities. I took the initiative to become certified through formal training offered by professional organizations, achieving multiple certifications.

Building Positive Relationships

I made a concerted effort to foster positive relationships with my boss and colleagues, recognizing the importance of a strong support system in the workplace. I remained mindful of not adopting any negative habits that could hinder my progress or tarnish my reputation. By maintaining a professional demeanor and demonstrating a willingness to collaborate, I built a network of allies invested in my success.

Being Vocal and Proactive

Participating in work rituals and seeking guidance when needed was vital. Rather than completing tasks in isolation, I engaged with my colleagues, asked questions, and contributed to discussions. This proactive approach helped me gain a deeper understanding of my role and the organization's operations and demonstrated my commitment to being an active and valuable team member.

Requesting Regular Feedback

To ensure continuous improvement, I made it a habit to request weekly feedback from my manager and colleagues. Actively seeking constructive criticism and insights into my performance allowed me to identify areas for growth and adjust my approach. This commitment to self-improvement benefited both me and my team.

Days 60–90

Starting to Contribute

As I settled into my routine and became more comfortable with my responsibilities, I sought ways to increase my contribution to the team and the organization. I actively sought opportunities to assist my colleagues and volunteered for important projects that aligned with my skills and interests. By taking the initiative, I demonstrated my commitment to the organization's success and positioned myself as a valuable asset.

Setting Boundaries

While being proactive and contributing was important, I learned the crucial lesson of setting boundaries to prevent burnout and maintain a healthy work-life balance. I recognized that overextending myself could lead to decreased productivity and job satisfaction in the long run. By establishing clear boundaries and communicating them effectively with my manager and colleagues, I prioritized my well-being while still meeting the demands of my role.

Taking Ownership of Career Development

As I approached the end of my first ninety days, I took a more active role in planning my career path within the organization. I sought advice from my manager on potential next steps and opportunities for growth, expressing my desire to take on additional responsibilities and develop new skills. By initiating these conversations and demonstrating a proactive approach to my professional development, I showcased my commitment to a long-term career with the organization.

90 Days and Beyond

Setting Long-Term Goals

Entering my fourth month, I worked closely with my manager to establish complex, long-term goals requiring detailed planning and execution. However, I faced unexpected challenges in career advancement. Despite my proactive approach and dedication, I was passed over for a supervisory position, which led to frustration and disappointment. This experience marked a turning point in my career, leading me to consider new opportunities.

Overcoming Setbacks and Disappointments

To my surprise and disappointment, I was passed over for a promotion in favor of someone with less experience and no degree. When I requested a review of the decision, I was told that my qualifications might lead me to seek opportunities elsewhere, leaving the organization hesitant to invest in my advancement. Despite my love for the job, this experience prompted me to explore other career opportunities.

Staying Vigilant and Preparing for New Opportunities

Amidst the disappointment, I noticed the increasing presence of job search platforms. I realized that in today's rapidly evolving job market, one must always be looking for the next opportunity. While remaining committed to my current role, I proactively explored potential career moves that aligned with my long-term goals and values.

Building a Personal Brand

Despite setbacks, I focused on creating a deliberate personal brand based on values like integrity, leadership, and dependability. I made a concerted effort to ensure these qualities were reflected in my daily work, interactions with colleagues, and contributions to the organization. By consistently demonstrating my value and potential, I aimed to position myself as a strong candidate for future opportunities.

Knowing When to Move On

As I navigated the challenges and disappointments of my career, I came to understand the importance of recognizing when it was time to move on. While I remained committed to my role and the organization, I also actively explored new opportunities that aligned with my long-term goals and values. Sometimes, the best path forward involves leaving a comfortable position in pursuit of growth and fulfillment elsewhere.

Preparing for Job Interviews

During my job search, I quickly learned that interviews for higher-level positions often involved panels consisting of different stakeholders. To prepare for these multifaceted interviews, I honed my communication skills, articulated my achievements and qualifications, and demonstrated my ability to collaborate effectively with diverse groups. By showcasing my adaptability and strategic thinking, I aimed to position myself as a strong candidate capable of driving positive change and contributing to organizational success.

Making the Most of Your Early Experience

Learn, Network, Communicate

Regardless of where you start, strive to become an expert on your organization, not just your specific role. Take the initiative to learn how different departments function and interrelate. Sit in on public meetings to observe decision-making and community engagement in action. Volunteer for additional duties and cross-functional projects to expand your skill set and internal network.

Improving Communication Skills

Hone your communication skills by interacting with colleagues, leaders, and the public. Practice distilling complex policies into clear, accessible language—a key skill in government work. Learn to write effective memos, reports, proposals, and public information materials. Observe how seasoned professionals navigate difficult conversations and aim to model their poise and focus on solutions.

Building a Professional Network

Start by building relationships where you are. Make office friends and mentors. Attend office lunches, take walking breaks with coworkers. For instance, building strong professional connections and seeking advice from trusted colleagues can be invaluable.

Join professional associations like Engaging Local Government Leaders (ELGL), International City/County Management Association (ICMA), or state/regional organizations. Attend conferences and workshops to learn from experts and meet peers in your field. Connect with mentors from inside and outside your organization who can offer guidance and make introductions that expand your opportunities.

Pursuing Graduate Education

This is also a good time to consider whether earning a graduate degree would accelerate your career goals. While a master of public administration (MPA), master of public policy (MPP), or similar degree isn't essential for advancement, especially early on, these programs provide valuable knowledge, skills, and networking. Many schools offer part-time, executive, and online formats if you want to pursue a degree while working. Employers may even offer tuition assistance.

Demonstrating Initiative

Find opportunities to practice leadership, even in small ways like organizing a volunteer project. Deliver quality, timely work to build your reputation. Learn from successes and stumbles. Stay attuned to issues facing your community and how your daily work fits into the bigger picture. Make your enthusiasm and commitment to public service visible. That's the foundation for early career success and future growth.

Managing Work-Life Balance

Balancing Personal and Professional Challenges

As I navigated my early career in local government, I faced numerous challenges both professionally and personally. I struggled with low pay and long hours, often working multiple jobs to support my young family. This period coincided with personal challenges, which took a significant emotional toll on me. Balancing the demands of work and family life was a constant struggle.

Respect and Fairness Win the Day

As a new employee, it's crucial to create an inclusive workplace while also ensuring you're treated fairly. To avoid prejudice, I started by examining my own biases. We all have them, often unconsciously. I took implicit bias tests online to uncover mine. I then actively worked to counter these biases in my interactions.

I made a conscious effort to treat everyone equally, regardless of their background. I listened to my colleagues, valuing their input based on merit rather than personal characteristics. I avoided making assumptions about people's abilities or interests based on stereotypes. I educated myself about different cultures, experiences, and perspectives. This can help you better understand and relate to diverse coworkers. If your company offers diversity training, participate enthusiastically.

Be mindful of your language. Avoid potentially offensive terms or jokes, even if you think they're harmless. If you make a mistake, apologize sincerely and learn from it.

To ensure you're treated fairly, know your rights. Familiarize yourself with your company's policies on discrimination and harassment, as well as relevant labor laws. Document your work and achievements. Keep a record of your contributions, positive feedback, and any issues that arise. This can be valuable if you ever need to address unfair treatment.

Build a strong professional network within your organization. Having allies can provide support and perspective if you face discrimination.

If you experience or witness unfair treatment, speak up. Use proper channels like HR or your supervisor to report issues. Be specific and factual in your complaints.

Lastly, remember that creating an inclusive workplace is everyone's responsibility. By modeling respectful behavior and standing up for fairness, you contribute to a positive environment for all.

Transitioning to a Supervisory Role

Embrace Leadership Challenges

Transitioning into a supervisory role was a significant milestone in my midcareer development. As a first-time supervisor, I had to learn to manage a diverse team, navigate complex personnel issues, and implement new programs effectively. Clear, unambiguous communication was crucial in establishing expectations and addressing performance issues.

Continue to Build Professional Relationships

Building strong professional relationships and seeking guidance from trusted colleagues was invaluable. My friendships with colleagues provided invaluable advice and support during challenging times. Don't hesitate to reach out to others in your field and cultivate these relationships.

Be a Proactive Problem Solver

I remained committed to continuous learning and proactive problem-solving. When I uncovered significant issues, I took the initiative to address them. Similarly, I developed new programs to improve community services, even in the face of political opposition.

Embrace Growth Opportunities

As you progress in your career, remember that challenges are opportunities for growth. Embrace them, learn from them, and stay true to your values and commitment to public service. The lessons you learn from these experiences will shape you into a stronger, more effective leader in the long run.

Keys to Success: Quality Work, Continuous Learning, Enthusiasm

Throughout my early career, I remained committed to hard work, delivering quality results, and continuously learning. I achieved certification across multiple levels of formal training and demonstrated initiative by developing new programs and pioneering processes. Despite the challenges of low pay and long hours, my enthusiasm for local government work never waned. These key factors contributed to my success and set the foundation for my future growth in the field.

Midlevel Management

Midcareer Leadership: Mastering the Art of Managing People, Projects, and Resources

As an emerging leader in local government, the focus shifts toward managing people, projects, and resources strategically to advance departmental and organizational objectives. It's a time to apply accumulated knowledge and stretch your skills in new ways, moving from individual contributor to manager.

Assessing and Reshaping Inherited Teams

In my career, I've often taken charge of existing teams rather than building them from scratch. This involves first thoroughly assessing the team's composition, capabilities, and challenges, then strategically reshaping roles and responsibilities while establishing clear operational processes. By securing early wins and building momentum, I've successfully led inherited teams to higher performance levels. Understanding the unique dynamics and thoughtfully implementing changes is key to effectively leading these teams.

Navigating the Transition to Leadership

Transitioning into a leadership role comes with misconceptions and challenges. The authority and autonomy I expected were tempered by the realities of navigating complex webs of relationships and competing demands. Building credibility with employees, peers, and superiors proved more critical than any formal position. Seeking guidance from mentors and remaining committed to continuous learning have been essential in my development as a leader. This journey, though challenging, is rewarding as it allows for significant personal and professional growth.

Creating a Sustainable High-Performance Culture

High-intensity work environments, with their relentless demands and constant connectivity, can take a toll on employees' well-being and productivity. As a leader, modeling and encouraging boundaries, prioritizing output over face time, and creating a culture that values sustainable performance are crucial. Implementing strategies like setting realistic expectations, promoting work-life balance, fostering open communication, and providing ample support and resources helps create a healthier and more engaged workforce.

Leveraging the Power of Persuasion

The principles of persuasion have been invaluable in my leadership journey. Understanding psychological factors like reciprocity, scarcity, authority, consistency, liking, and consensus enhances my ability to communicate effectively and drive change. Whether negotiating with stakeholders, rallying my team around a vision, or making a case for resources, employing these principles strategically has been a game changer. Building credibility, leveraging social proof, and creating a sense of shared purpose helps persuade others to buy into ideas and initiatives, advancing organizational goals.

Cultivating Emotional Intelligence

Emotional intelligence has been transformative in my leadership development. Self-awareness, self-regulation, motivation, empathy, and social skills are essential for managing my emotions, building trusting relationships, inspiring others, and navigating challenges. Emotional intelligence is not a fixed trait but a set of skills that can be developed over time with concerted effort and practice. Embracing this growth mindset has been a cornerstone of my leadership development.

Supporting New Managers' Success

Transitioning from individual contributor to manager can be a struggle. The shift in responsibilities, coupled with insecurities and reluctance to ask for help, can lead rookie managers to flounder. As a senior leader, I prioritize anticipating these challenges and providing necessary support and guidance. Addressing common pitfalls—delegating effectively, seeking assistance, projecting confidence, thinking strategically, and delivering constructive feedback—helps set new managers up for success, driving overall performance.

Addressing Toxic Behavior

Dealing with toxic employees is an unfortunate reality of leadership. Spotting warning signs early, such as bullying or undermining behavior, allows for timely intervention. Documenting problems, providing clear feedback, and offering support while holding the employee accountable have guided me through difficult conversations. When necessary, making the tough call to let toxic employees go focuses on protecting the team's well-being and productivity. Effectively managing toxic employees is a critical leadership skill.

Coaching Underperforming Employees

Coaching struggling employees begins with identifying the root cause of performance issues. Tailoring the approach, providing targeted training, setting clear goals, and offering personalized support are essential steps. Regular check-ins and feedback sessions help monitor progress and make adjustments. Celebrating improvements reinforces positive changes. Investing time in helping underperformers succeed unlocks their potential and strengthens the team.

Navigating Challenging Personalities

Encountering stubborn, defensive, or defiant employees requires calm and composed leadership. Open, honest communication and understanding the employee's perspective often uncover underlying reasons for resistance. Setting clear expectations, providing support and resources, and focusing on specific behaviors rather than personal attacks help navigate tricky conversations. Documenting issues and involving HR may be necessary. Approaching these employees with empathy and a solutions-oriented mindset often turns situations around.

Breaking the "Set-Up-To-Fail" Cycle

Avoiding the "set-up-to-fail" trap involves recognizing warning signs and reflecting on managerial behavior. Micromanagement and lack of trust can erode an employee's confidence, leading to failure. Breaking this cycle requires resetting expectations, providing targeted support, and focusing on strengths and successes. Creating a positive, trusting environment fosters employee growth and success.

Recognizing and Addressing "Quiet Firing"

"Quiet firing" is a subtle form of workplace marginalization with serious consequences. Being aware of signs like exclusion from meetings or vague feedback without clear guidance is crucial. Addressing the situation involves open conversations, understanding employee perspectives, and developing improvement plans. Confronting biases and unfair treatment within the team or organization is necessary. Proactively identifying and addressing quiet firing creates an inclusive workplace culture.

Evaluating Bad Hires

Deciding whether to fire a bad hire involves objective assessment of performance, potential, and fit within the team. Identifying root causes, weighing costs and benefits, and considering solutions short of termination are key steps. If performance does not improve despite genuine efforts, making the difficult decision to let the employee go may be necessary. Learning from the experience refines the hiring process to avoid similar missteps.

Making Sound Termination Decisions

Terminating an employee requires careful consideration and a systematic approach. Gathering data on performance and behavior, identifying root causes, and considering costs and benefits are essential. Seeking input from HR and legal stakeholders ensures fairness and compliance. If performance does not improve despite efforts, parting ways may be necessary. Approaching the situation with care, objectivity, and a commitment to learning and improvement balances individual and organizational needs.

Conducting Compassionate Terminations

Terminating an employee can be done with sensitivity and profession-alism. Preparing logistically and emotionally, choosing an appropriate time and place, and anticipating reactions are important. Being direct, honest, and empathetic during the conversation, offering support, and planning for team communication minimize negative impacts. Han-dling terminations with care and kindness makes a difficult experience less painful.

Handling Necessary Dismissals

Letting an employee go requires professionalism and empathy. Ensur-ing the decision is justified and documentation is in order is the first step. Being direct, honest, and respectful during the conversation, offer-ing support, and communicating with the team are crucial. Handling dismissals with care and compassion minimizes negative impacts on in-dividuals and the organization.

Letting Go of Strong Performers Due to Circumstances

Letting go of good employees due to factors beyond their control, such as restructuring, is challenging. Transparency and empathy throughout the process are key. Communicating reasons clearly, offering support, and managing team impact demonstrate care for the employee's well-being and future success. Handling the situation with sensitivity and respect helps good employees transition with dignity.

Developing as a Public Sector Manager

Moving into management requires a new mindset and skill set. Think-ing strategically, inspiring and guiding a team, and collaborating cross-functionally to solve problems are essential. Cultivating skills like strategic planning, effective communication, and team development are crucial.

Translating High-Level Directives into Clear Plans

Breaking down high-level directives into specific, measurable, and achievable goals and clearly communicating these objectives to the team are essential. Collaborating with the team to develop detailed action plans and assigning responsibilities based on strengths ensure everyone understands their role.

Delegating Effectively

Balancing guidance and autonomy in delegation involves clear communication of expectations, deadlines, and desired outcomes. Providing necessary resources and support while allowing team members to approach tasks in their own way and regularly checking in without micromanaging fosters effective delegation.

Developing and Coaching Staff

Tailoring coaching and development approaches to individual needs and learning styles is crucial. Providing structured guidance and frequent feedback for less experienced staff and encouraging more experienced team members to mentor others fosters a culture of continuous learning and growth.

Managing Budgets and Resources

Prioritizing initiatives that align with the organization's mission and provide the greatest public value is key to effective budget and resource management. Regular monitoring and analysis of spending, identifying cost savings, and fostering partnerships enhance efficiency and maximize public value.

Facilitating Productive Discussions

Creating an inclusive environment where all team members feel heard and valued is essential for productive discussions. Defining the purpose and goals, keeping conversations focused, encouraging diverse perspectives, and maintaining a respectful tone are crucial. Making decisions based on available information and potential impacts ensures effective decision-making.

Negotiating and Resolving Conflicts

Approaching negotiations and conflicts with empathy and a focus on mutually beneficial solutions is essential. Active listening, identifying common ground, brainstorming creative solutions, and maintaining a calm demeanor help resolve conflicts constructively.

Presenting to Senior Leaders

Thorough research, clear and concise presentation of findings, and tailoring communication to the audience are essential when presenting to senior leaders. Anticipating questions, providing thoughtful responses, and offering actionable recommendations based on expertise and analysis ensure effective presentations.

Continuing to Pursue Training and Development

Actively pursuing training and development opportunities through professional associations like the American Planning Association and the

International City/County Management Association (ICMA) enhances skills and knowledge. Community leadership programs and mentoring relationships further support professional growth.

Building Cross-Functional Understanding and Relationships

Collaborating with colleagues across departments and understanding local government components and interactions are essential. Building relationships with peers and observing effective leaders navigate the organization broadens perspective and fosters cooperation.

Driving Change and Innovation

Identifying areas for improvement and leading change within your sphere of influence are crucial. Analyzing problems methodically, proposing data-driven solutions, piloting new approaches, and evaluating results objectively drive innovation. Encouraging smart risk-taking and consulting experts support effective change leadership.

Leading Change Effectively

Leading change effectively requires framing proposals around organizational priorities, anticipating concerns, and proactively addressing them. Clear communication, seeking feedback, and making adjustments ensure successful change implementation. Patience and persistence are key.

Preparing for Executive Roles

As you gain experience and prove your leadership abilities, envisioning a path to executive positions becomes natural. Seeking high-profile assignments, managing significant projects, and demonstrating grace under pressure build a reputation as a reliable problem-solver. Leadership opportunities outside the organization and professional associations further enhance visibility and skills.

Political Climate

Navigating political challenges and building support for new initiatives are essential for effective leadership. Engaging stakeholders, presenting data-driven arguments, and leveraging support from colleagues help overcome obstacles. Ethical leadership and careful consideration of organizational culture are critical.

Mentoring and Sponsorship

Mentoring relationships support professional growth and advancement. Seeking guidance from respected managers and learning from their experiences enhance leadership development.

Rounding Out Skills and Experience

Proactively seeking opportunities to round out skills in budgeting, personnel management, and community engagement prepares for executive roles. Lateral moves and certifications bolster credibility. Strategic planning, mentoring, and individual development plans support career advancement.

Throughout my journey as a mid-level manager, I have learned that success in local government requires a combination of technical expertise, leadership skills, and the ability to build relationships and drive change. By actively pursuing professional development, taking on challenging assignments, and learning from mentors and colleagues, I have continued to grow and prepare myself for the next stage of my career. While the path has not always been easy, I remain committed to serving my community and making a positive impact through my work in local government.

Executive Leadership in Local Government: Guiding Communities to Success

As an executive leader in local government—whether a department head, assistant city manager, or city manager—your responsibility is to steer the organization strategically, marshal resources, build an outstanding team, and deliver maximum value to the community. This role is both a weighty responsibility and an extraordinary opportunity to shape the future of a place and touch many lives.

Improve Performance against Agency Mission

Public-sector organizations must focus on promoting the public's welfare. Effective execution of their mission motivates agency staffers. Leaders must rededicate their commitment to the mission, establish clear performance-improvement goals, and formulate specific initiatives to address performance or skills gaps.

Identifying structural inefficiencies and outdated policies is essential for modernizing an organization. Addressing organizational bloat and inefficient staffing principles can involve recommending a multiyear reorganization plan, eliminating excess positions, and downsizing the workforce. This approach aims to streamline operations and enhance the agency's ability to meet its mission effectively.

\\\

The Trail to Success

Win over Stakeholders

Agency heads must cultivate a wide range of stakeholders, both external and internal. External stakeholders need to understand the agency's capabilities and value. Internal stakeholders, particularly long-term employees, possess valuable operational knowledge, and their support is crucial for successful change. Training programs and incentives can help address skill deficiencies and lack of will among employees.

Gaining internal insights and support from department directors before finalizing reorganization strategies can help avoid unnecessary resistance. Engaging with the community through various platforms and building relationships with staff, council members, business owners, organization leaders, and local residents is essential. This engagement fosters trust and facilitates the successful implementation of change.

Create a Road Map

A change effort road map generally has three major phases: identify performance objectives, set priorities, and roll out the program. A change team should identify areas requiring urgent attention and outline obstacles to reform. Prioritization should consider the impact on performance and the difficulty of implementation. Quick wins help generate faith in long-term change efforts. Rollout should begin in receptive areas and gradually extend to other offices.

Implementing a phased approach to restructuring, targeting the elimination of dispensable positions, and downsizing the workforce can streamline operations. Despite political maneuvering, gaining council approval for such proposals through separate votes on each position signals majority support for crucial new roles.

Take a Comprehensive Approach

For organizations to perform at a superior level, leadership, structure, processes, infrastructure, people, and performance management must be integrated and aligned. Adopting a comprehensive approach may require integrating activities across organizational boundaries.

Navigating political power dynamics within the council structure involves developing political capital with influential members beyond just the mayor. Understanding complex interpersonal histories and power relations is essential for advancing key initiatives.

Be a Leader, Not a Bureaucrat

Change leaders must find ways to see over and around barriers, not simply knock them over. Political appointees must convince stakeholders of their sincerity and commitment to improving performance against the mission. When objectives are clear and meaningful change is undertaken, agencies can achieve their highest purpose.

Promoting organizational change includes introducing initiatives such as outfitting officers with body-worn cameras for accountability and transparency. During crises, such as officer-involved shootings, providing clear and timely communication and engaging with the community are crucial for maintaining public trust.

Charting a Strategic Vision

Local government executives must be visionary leaders, always scanning the horizon for emerging opportunities, challenges, and trends that will impact their community. Synthesizing these inputs into a clear, compelling vision for the organization focused on service, effectiveness, and innovation is vital. Engaging the team in strategic planning to assess current strengths, weaknesses, and performance gaps sets the stage for achieving ambitious but achievable goals.

Communicating the vision at every opportunity and aligning every initiative to that vision builds a culture of purpose with the North Star of public service at the center. Providing both direction and space for the team to achieve results, delegating authority, giving people stretch assignments, and fostering an environment where new ideas are encouraged are essential leadership practices.

Driving Operational Excellence

Managing multimillion-dollar budgets is a huge responsibility and a constant puzzle. There are always worthy programs and critical needs that outstrip available funds. A keen understanding of revenue sources, cost drivers, legal obligations, and long-term forecasts is essential. Thinking creatively about how to maximize and stretch resources through efficiencies, partnerships, and judicious risk-taking is crucial.

Operational excellence involves championing a data-driven, performance-oriented culture. Investing in integrated systems for tracking key metrics, establishing performance measures that cascade through the organization, and regularly reviewing dashboards for insights are essential practices. Improving processes and programs based on evidence, empowering staff to initiate improvements, and spotlighting successes are vital for continuous improvement.

Harnessing technology to streamline work, enhance service, and engage the public in new ways is another critical aspect of driving operational excellence. Staying abreast of government technology innovations and evaluating what tools could take operations to the next level is essential.

Navigating Political Dynamics

Local government executives must be adept at navigating political currents while maintaining trust and stability. Councils and commissions are made up of people with diverse backgrounds, personalities, and agendas. Building positive, productive relationships with each member is an art and a necessity.

Being a reliable, objective advisor to elected officials involves providing unvarnished analysis and recommendations, respecting their authority as policymakers, and being transparent about successes, challenges, and options. Adapting communication styles to each official's preferences and understanding what drives each of them are crucial for building effective relationships.

Staying above the political fray publicly, avoiding any perception of favoritism, and upholding strong ethical standards are essential practices. Using public funds prudently, disclosing potential conflicts of interest, and being consistent in applying policies maintain integrity and trust.

Leading through Crisis

Leading through crises requires clear-eyed assessment, decisive action, and empathetic communication. During challenging times, such as officer-involved shootings or the COVID-19 pandemic, providing steady, principled leadership that prioritizes transparency, empathy, and the well-being of the community is crucial.

Engaging directly with community stakeholders, advocating for necessary resources, and taking decisive action to protect public health and safety are essential practices. These experiences demonstrate the importance of staying true to values, prioritizing community needs, and working collaboratively with stakeholders to guide cities through challenging times.

Engaging the Community

As a local government executive, you're not just a leader within the walls of city hall but a steward of the entire community. Effective two-way communication with residents, businesses, and community organizations is essential for understanding and meeting public needs, building trust, and fostering shared ownership of the community's future.

Engaging the public across a variety of methods, communicating in clear, accessible language, and telling authentic stories of impact are crucial practices. Using disaggregated data to understand how different segments of the community are faring and guiding equitable investments helps address disparities in outcomes.

Making engagement everyone's job, training staff in cultural competence and customer service, and empowering residents with open data and tools for community improvement are essential strategies. Proactive, transparent, and empathetic communication during crises or controversies helps maintain trust and focus on solutions and community resilience.

Your Development as a Leader

Even as you reach the upper echelons of your career, you're never done growing as a leader. Investing in your continued development is essential for avoiding burnout, sharpening your skills for new challenges, and role-modeling the importance of lifelong learning.

Regularly exposing yourself to new ideas from other sectors and disciplines, pursuing structured leadership development programs, and engaging in executive coaching can help you gain self-awareness, navigate interpersonal dynamics, and lead transformative change. Building a diverse personal board of advisors and participating in peer networks provide vital support and challenge your assumptions.

Understanding and adapting to the unique cultural norms, values, and power dynamics of the communities you serve while maintaining professional integrity and expertise is crucial. Overcoming adversity, such as smear campaigns and disinformation, requires focusing on building trust through consistent action, delivering results, and maintaining integrity in the face of challenges.

Reflecting on these challenges and responsibilities, local government executives must remain committed to answering the call of public service with dedication and resilience. The path may be difficult, but the reward of making a positive difference in the lives of those we serve is unparalleled.

ABOUT HOWARD W. BROWN JR.

HOWARD W. BROWN, JR. has been appointed the first Black city manager in three cities. He is an alum of Harvard University, University of West Florida, and Florida State University. Brown is a member of Omega Psi Phi Fraternity, Inc. The father of two lives in Florida with his wife.